Praise for *The Happy Empty Nest*

"Universities and colleges should provide this book in the orientation package they send to parents. The information is practical and just enough to trigger further exploration rather than being overwhelming."

—JACQUELINE I. HAINES, director, the Gesell Institute for Human Development

"This book tells you how the time you have now, when your kids are in college, can be the best of times. Enjoy your spouse, get to see your kids in a whole new light, travel, read, grow. Very well written, insightful, filled with the tools to make this the best time of your life."

—MARY BETH CAREY, vice president for Enrollment Services, Hofstra University

The Happy Empty Nest is a comprehensive, thoughtful, practical book written in an engaging and supportive style. I highly recommend it to people during this significant developmental transition."

—ERICA RAPPORT, Ph.D., psychologist

The Happy Empty Nest offers a much-needed roadmap for parents to negotiate through the wonderful, confusing, surprising and ultimately rewarding empty nest years. Linda Burghardt's insightful ideas are comforting for parents who feel a sense of void, and cajoling for those who aren't sure what to do. When the kids head off for college, make this book your first stop on a journey of discovery and rejuvenation."

—JAMIE MERSOTIS, president, the Institute for Higher Education Policy

"Linda Burghardt's guide for parents on how to enhance both their own lives and that of their children is replete with wise advice for turning the empty-nest syndrome into an opportunity for loving, learning, and experimenting that was not attainable while raising a family. I recommend *The Happy Empty Nest* to all parents of college (and beyond) children."

—HOWARD GREENE, nationally known college placement counselor, former admissions officer at Princeton University and author of *Making It Into a Top College* and *Scaling the Ivy Walls in the '90s.*

"A terrific resource for empty nesters—practical, readable, and very informative. It challenges parents to make the most of those exciting years and provides the necessary tools to do so."

—JOHNNE ARMENTROUT, M.A., director, Wake Forest University Counseling Center, and coordinator, Empty Nest Program for WFU Parents of Freshmen

"An excellent guide for parents whose children are flying from the nest. Well-written, with sensible advice, encouragement, and exercises for re-establishing couplehood, and wise advice for just-right parenting of children who are becoming adults."

—TINE B. TESSINA, Ph.D., family psychotherapist and author of *How to Be a Couple and Still Be Free* and *The Ten Smartest Decisions a Woman Can Make After Forty*

"An authoritative, well-written, interesting guide to refeathering the empty nest. Newcomers, or soon-to-be-inhabitants, will find it invaluable—even long-term empty nesters will find it useful."

—SYLVIA AUERBACH, author of *How to Be Smart Parents Now That Your Kids Are Adults*

"The Happy Empty Nest is a delightful and informative guide for parents who have had plenty of advice about their children's college education but little or no support for their own new stage in life. It is practical, useful, and inspiring. Empty nesters will find encouragement in the recognition that their feelings and experiences are not unique but universal. There is life after the room deposit is made and tuition payments begin. And those who follow Linda Burghardt's advice will find it a very rich and rewarding life."

—JACOB LUDES, III, executive director and CEO, New England Association of Schools and Colleges

"This author brings up big topics and gets readers involved. Important issues . . . valuable advice . . . real-world dialogue."

—JOAN DETZ, author of *It's Not What You Say, It's How You Say It*

"The Happy Empty Nest provides guidance for the new roles that parents take on once their child has gone on to college. Linda Burghardt really understands the new family dynamic. Read the book with care, read it with a sense of humor, read it with an open mind, and you'll realize that sending a child off to college can be liberating—for the entire family."

—JOAN ISAAC MOHR, vice president and dean of Admissions, Quinnipiac University

The
Happy
Empty Nest

The
Happy
Empty Nest

Rediscovering Love and Success
After Your Kids Leave Home

Linda Burghardt

CITADEL PRESS
Kensington Publishing Corp.
www.kensingtonbooks.com

CITADEL PRESS BOOKS are published by

Kensington Publishing Corp.
850 Third Avenue
New York, NY 10022

All Kensington titles, imprints, and distributed lines are available at special quantity discounts for bulk purchases for sales promotions, premiums, fund-raising, educational, or institutional use. Special book excerpts or customized printings can also be created to fit specific needs. For details, write or phone the office of the Kensington special sales manager: Kensington Publishing Corp., 850 Third Avenue, New York, NY 10022, attn: Special Sales Department, phone 1-800-221-2647.

CITADEL PRESS is Reg. U.S. Pat. & TM Off.
The Citadel Logo is a trademark of Kensington Publishing Corp.

First printing: October 2002

10 9 8 7 6 5 4 3 2 1

Printed in the United States of America

Library of Congress Control Number: 2002104523

ISBN 0-8065-2401-4

To my husband, David,
and our twin daughters,
Katie and Amy

CONTENTS

Contents

PREFACE

What were your wishes and dreams before your children were born? Did you interrupt your education when you became a parent? Trade an adventurous career for a safe one? Channel your resources into your family's growth instead of your own?

If you are like most parents, you found you had no choice but to direct your time, money, and energy into your kids. But now that those kids have left home for college, you have the opportunity to use those resources in a new and wonderful way—for your own development. In other words, you have the chance to go back and revisit who you were before the children came, tap into those dreams, and make a plan to fulfill them.

Even if raising your kids has been the most fulfilling part of your life so far, you will find that even better years are about to begin. This book will show you how to make them happen, not by examining how you feel—you already know that—but by showing you how to take action. Step by step it will enable you to navigate successfully through the social, emotional, cultural, philosophical, and financial changes that are inevitable when children leave home. It will guide you through the maze of opportunities that accompany these changes, so that you can renew your sense of purpose and create the kind of life for yourself that will give you lasting challenge and fulfillment.

This is a book for all parents—for stay-at-homes and breadwinners, single parents, and married partners, whether you are empty-nested in your early forties or late sixties, live a life on the fast track, or embrace one of voluntary simplicity. It's about what you can do to define your place in the world and make sure it is a good one, one you choose and not an unsatisfying role assigned to you by a seemingly indifferent society.

As children make the transition from bedroom to dorm room, they instinctively learn to distinguish between mere motion and useful progress. The lucky ones become accustomed to the ground shifting beneath their feet and master the dance steps that enable them to move with it. But not all parents adapt as readily to the world of growth and second chances that opens up to them when their last child leaves home and the hours in the day become their own once again.

Empty nests look very different from the outside than they do when you've been in them for awhile. From the hundreds of college parents I interviewed for this book and the stories they shared with me, one theme emerged: The parents who came through it best were those who saw it not as an end but as a transition to a new stage of parenthood. The most successful instinctively understood that the best way to insure that our children would happily embrace their future was to successfully reach out toward our own.

This book will show you how. We will examine the plethora of issues about family life that change in this time of transition: what gets better, what gets worse, and how to improve both; what the experts recommend; what new opportunities become available and how to use them to your advantage; how to plot your growth and support your goals with new and rediscovered resources.

Together we will look at love, fun, friendship, finances, parenting, and career paths. We will discuss health, the home environment, education, community activism, and travel. We will talk about privacy, changing values, freedom, security, and much more.

Although the book is written specifically for college parents, the transition they are going through is universal; all parents share similar experiences when their last child moves away from home. So if your son or daughter has left the nest to start a career or to join the Peace Corps or other government service, this book is also for you.

So take the quizzes. Consider the advice. Study the choices. When you are ready, dust off your dreams, give yourself permission to follow them and create your game plan to do so. You will enjoy your trip back into familiar territory. And when you get there, perhaps you will have discovered the best-kept secret of all—that the empty nest does not stay empty for long, but soon fills quite happily once again with nurturing relationships, deeply satisfied family members, and the wealth of resources you need to make your dreams come alive.

ACKNOWLEDGMENTS

Like artists applying the defining brushstrokes to their paintings, many people have left their indelible imprint on the pages of this book. It is my privilege to thank them all here.

To Margaret Wolf, my friend and colleague, I offer my appreciation for her creative guidance, for suggesting the idea of this book to me, and for her outstanding editing. I deeply appreciate the efforts of Elizabeth Wissner-Gross and my sister-in-law Betsy Gibson Pierce for helping to make the college experience richer than we dared to dream. Thanks are offered to the administrative offices at both Princeton University and Yale University for answering my unending stream of questions.

I offer my gratitude to the devoted staff at the Great Neck Library in Great Neck, New York, for all their help in my research, and my sincere thanks go to my agent, Sheree Bykofsky, for exercising her good business sense on my behalf. To Bruce Bender and the hard-working staff at Kensington Books I offer gratitude for their willingness to make bookmaking such a joy.

Much love and appreciation go to Mary Wynperle, Bobbie Preiser, Charlotte Lee, and Jill Danzig Tarlow, fellow travelers in the fields and forests of motherhood, for their insights and the sharing that has taught me so much. And I am most fortunate to have received a lifetime of loving guidance from my own parents, Hilda and Fred Feuerberg.

To my husband, David, my partner in parenting, I offer my deepest gratitude for the beauty of his spirit and for his unerring belief in me, and to our daughters, Katie, Yale '05, and Amy, Princeton '05, I give thanks for the love that makes everything else possible.

PART I

Love in a Time
of Transition

Chapter One

STARTING OVER
AS A COUPLE

The last trunk has been lugged into the dorm room, the last reading lamp assembled, the coveted top bunk covered with the brand-new extra-long quilt. The roommates have already left for the first freshman orientation meeting, and your child is flushed with excitement, feet already pointed toward the door, nervously eager to enter the mystery that is college.

You hug and release and hug again, grasping sweaty palms, patting shoulders that seem both newly large and achingly frail at the same time. You know you should head for the car but your feet feel pasted to the floor. Then someone is at your elbow, guiding you on those first steps down the long corridor. You turn for one last look over your shoulder, but your eager freshman has already melted into the throng of identically T-shirted students, newly released into a world where everything is shiny new, everyone holds the promise of adventure, and nothing includes you.

Suddenly, you are alone with your spouse.

You walk to the car, tentatively brushing hands, wondering what to say, where to start, afraid that kind words will bring tears, equally afraid that the wrong words will stifle the tears before they form and trap them inside forever.

Before putting the key in the ignition, you look at one another for a long moment. Perhaps you see the person with whom a heart was shared in the long-ago days before the children came and realize for the first time that the sharing of the heart was what made the children possible in the first place. Maybe you see a reflection of your next self in your spouse's eyes, a person still fuzzy around the edges but already dashing into unknown territory, already reaching toward the opportunity to pick up growing where it was left off when the children came.

In a way you feel you are looking backward and forward at the same time, glimpsing a vision of the future that is within your power to grasp. But to realize its gains, you need a plan, a roadmap of sorts, an honest heart and more courage than it took even to send your child out of your home and into the world—in other words, far more courage than you believe you have.

But the truth is otherwise; you already possess everything you need for this next stage of life. You need only stop and look at where you are to see that now is a time to take stock, assess your plans, and attempt, in light of all that will change now that your last child is out of the house, to define your wishes. Now is a chance that will never come again.

The Five Tasks of Marriage

Marriage counselors and other therapists who work with couples differ widely in technique when it comes to helping create a stable, happy relationship, but they uniformly agree that there are five major tasks that couples need to accomplish to make a serious, lasting relationship thrive. Couples need to learn to trust one another, laugh together, develop intimacy, resolve power struggles, and support one another's goals.

The good news is that all these tasks can be accomplished with good will and hard work. The bad news is that stress aggravates each and every one of them and makes them into pressure points that can weaken the bonds that hold couples together. Having your last child leave home is definitely a major stressor, and each area in a relationship is bound to look different to you the day after your child moves out of the upstairs bedroom and into the dorm.

What can you do? A good place to start is to take a look at the five tasks and determine how the stress of finding yourself alone with your partner is likely to affect them. In every case, there is the potential for trouble to develop, but clinging closely to the back of trouble is the opportunity for new and deeper happiness. It is not simple to try to build a different kind of marriage in the midst of overwhelming change, but a deeper and better relationship at this risky stage of life can be the basis for a new level of joy, growth, and intimacy.

WHAT THE EXPERTS SAY ABOUT MARRIAGE

"In every study in which Americans are asked what they value most in assessing the quality of their lives, marriage comes first—ahead of friends, jobs and money. In our fast-paced world, men and women seem to need each other more, not less."

—*Judith Wallerstein, clinical psychologist*

"In today's society, you are encouraged to view marriage as a box. First you choose your mate. Then you climb into a box. In other words, marriage is viewed as an unchanging state. But marriage is not a static state between two people. Marriage is a psychological and spiritual journey."

—*Harville Hendrix, marriage therapist*

Creating More Togetherness

Children are great buffers in a marriage. Without them in the house, issues you thought were settled years ago can sneak back up to the surface again and bite you in places you didn't even remember you had. Some couples find that before they can enjoy the energizing freedoms that characterize the empty nest, they need to face the unresolved conflicts that have somehow found a way to stay alive for as many years as their children have been in the house.

This is not easy to do, to say the least; many of these are issues that have continued to exert influence over your life despite the fact that they have managed to stay hidden. Thus the first step toward resolving them is to bring them to the surface, a place they do not want to be because they will lose power. Be prepared for a fight; you will have to drag them up.

Fortunately, couples without children in the house enjoy an ideal situation for working out their differences. Time to spend together is more abundant than before. Privacy, wonderful privacy, exists once again. Spaces in the house that used to be available to you only on an occasional basis are now open to you round the clock. But most important, couples have no one else at home to go to with their feelings, and sooner or later that is bound to create the perfect atmosphere for them to begin to express these feelings to each other.

Some couples set a weekly date to share plans and bring up issues; others talk when the feelings come out and try to stick to the goal of resolution until it is achieved. In either case, often the very act of working to resolve differences serves to bring the two partners closer together. Frequently it represents the first time they have had the opportunity to spend time discussing their own issues and not their children's, and this in itself is a bonding process.

In the best of circumstances, time spent together can remind a couple of why they were attracted to one another in the first place. In the busy years of raising children at home, there is rarely time to look closely at one's spouse; now, in the aftermath of the last child's leave-taking, often the moment presents itself when those early feelings have a chance to be rekindled. Allow them to occur! Often the result is more togetherness, a happy outcome that not only aids in the process of conflict resolution, but also lays the groundwork for a new kind of intimacy.

Hidden Barriers to Love

In the early days of marriage, the task of coming together as partners is often more difficult than anticipated, not because the bride and groom do not love each other sufficiently or fail to fully believe in the goodness of their union, but because they are often not entirely free to give themselves to one another. Few newlyweds realize that until they separate sufficiently from their parents they cannot bond fully with their spouse. In the first year or two after the walk down the aisle, a great many conflicts that arise have this unseen problem at their basis.

For parents whose children have grown up and left home, the task of separating in order to come together again is often hampered by a different lack of freedom—ties to children that prevent a full bonding with a spouse or partner. Our society does not fully acknowledge the deep connections we often feel for children of this age, telling us quite plainly that their leaving home is a normal life passage to which the left-behind parents should easily adjust.

But conversations with bereft parents tell a different story entirely. Grieving accompanies the process of accepting the departure of a grown child far more frequently that we like to admit. For women especially, but also for a great number of men, the knowledge that one's major parenting years are over can bring about a deep sadness that often leads to full-fledged depression. We can easily convince ourselves that our children's departure has made us worthless.

But the truth is the facts of modern life say otherwise. For one thing we live so much longer than we used to, and our childbearing and child-raising years comprise only a fraction of our useful adulthood. For another, many Americans today enjoy a second career or even a third in their lifetimes. But all this can seem like mere words when the key emotion we are feeling, our grief, remains unacknowledged.

Rituals for Renewal

One very effective way to counter this is to work openly with your spouse to bring this issue to the fore. Our society has many deeply embedded rituals for life's major passages—birth, coming-of-age, religious commitment, graduation, marriage—why not a ceremony to mark this important transition? It is not difficult to create your own custom-made ritual once you understand its purpose, and a ceremony of this nature can go a long way toward giving form and structure to your painful emotions, thus freeing you from revisiting the loss and giving you strength to begin the next stage of life.

First, think about the purpose of ritual: how it helps us acknowledge change, mark the value of a transition, and enable us to move on. Next, define the elements that make a ritual successful: a supportive atmosphere, words and acts of healing, a sense of release and letting go.

To create your own ritual to honor your child's transition, you may want to invite close friends or family to a small ceremony at your home, setting up a special place either indoors or outside in a garden or park. Some families gather pictures of their children and put them on a table decorated with candles and flowers, then ask guests to talk about the years they spent with them while they were growing up.

Other couples plant a tree in honor of their child's passage into the next stage of independence and maturity, gathering friends and family outside to talk about their hopes and expectations for that child. You might even tie a ribbon around the tree and ceremoniously cut it, thus symbolically cutting your ties with the earlier stages of your child's life. Or perhaps you and your spouse would find it useful to write your memories of your child's life thus far, read them to each other in private, and put them away in a special box.

As you make the break, you will find the energy you need to let go and move on to the next stage of your own life, the stage in which you, and not your child, are at the center of your world, with all your resources focused on your own happiness and well-being. In time your sadness will be replaced with hope and your grief with tenderness and memory. This is when your new, creative life can really begin.

The Gift of Time

All of us start our marriages hoping to create a committed relationship that will be central to our happiness, a union that will support our needs and increase in both strength and scope as the years go by. But when things go wrong we are often at a loss as to how to get back on track. We know how to build our house of love when our foundation is firm, yet a crumbling foundation is another story. With good luck, good finances, and good health, we learned how to build a wall of insulation around our marriages. But the very act of our children leaving home can send seismic shocks through a marriage.

If all the passion, energy, and excitement seems to have gone out of your relationship along with the children, you have to ask yourself whether you want to heal the marriage or abandon it and start over somewhere else. For many people the answer is clear; for others the quest to find out can begin an important process of self-discovery. In either case, this is work you must do by yourself before confronting your spouse.

For those who want to commit themselves to making a troubled marriage work, there are many no-nonsense, straightforward strategies that can help you understand your pain and problems and guide you toward eliminating them. Beginning couples therapy as soon as possible gives you the best chance to save your relationship. But if, on the other hand, the decision to end your marriage and start over again elsewhere is the one you are sure you want, it is in your best interest to take no action for at least six months.

The simple truth is that the shock and pain of children leaving home changes in quality and intensity as time passes, though this may not seem probable or even possible to you in the first few days or weeks after the event. Relationship counselors will be quick to tell you that the old canard about marrying in haste and repenting at leisure is unfortunately even more true about divorce.

RESOURCES AT YOUR FINGERTIPS

Over the years a great many books have been written about good marriages, offering everything from advice about how to strengthen the bond and make it better to guidance on how to put the laughter and romance back in your relationship when it seems to have gone flat. Here are three of the best of them:

Love, Honor and Negotiate: Making Your Marriage Work, by Betty Carter and Joan Peters, Simon & Schuster, 1996. A terrific how-to manual for working through differences to enable you to reach understanding and increased power in your marriage.

Soul Mates: Honoring the Mysteries of Love and Relationships, by Thomas Moore, HarperCollins, 1994. This book takes you on a journey through the spiritual aspects of personal unions and shows you the beauty that can be achieved. By the author of *Care of the Soul*.

The Seven Principles for Making Marriage Work, by John Gottman and Nan Silver, Three Rivers Press, 2000. You will find this step-by-step guide for a happy marriage extremely useful as a workbook to keep your relationship developing smoothly or as a reference when problems arise.

Marriage experts are fond of telling us that great relationships require great problem-solving skills, and they are right; but even more important is that relationships require a degree of emotional honesty that few of us can attain without a great deal of effort. Fortunately, when the children leave the nest the time and space to share private thoughts is suddenly restored to us, and those who want to make the effort find themselves with the happy opportunity to do so.

Certainly the house may be missing the noise and clamor of the rowdy adolescents who used to fill it up, but what is also missing are the intrusions and interruptions and the inhibitions about sharing your intimate space. Fill that space with your own lives for six months before making any decision about dismantling your marriage. Then do your self-discovery work again and see if the drive to leave is still as strong. The opportunity to rebuild a marriage is most dramatic just after your children leave home, but the window stays open forever. It is your choice whether, and when, to use it.

Relationship Workshop: The Anniversary Review

Once a year, on the same date every year if you can arrange it, sit down with your partner in a comfortable, private place. It is time to work on your relationship in a quiet and loving way. Choose a date that has meaning to you—your wedding day, the anniversary of the day you met, the day you first learned you would become parents. Surround yourselves with pillows, wine, soft music, anything that will help you relax. You are each going to have the chance to evaluate how your relationship has gone this past year, think about where you want it to go next year, and tell your partner your feelings.

Bring along a notebook and a pen for each of you. Some couples like to sit facing each other across a table, others find sitting side by side on the sofa to be best. You can recline on the floor or put your feet up in easy chairs. The important thing is to open your notebook to a clean page and try to answer each of these questions as honestly as possible:

1. Did I feel nurtured by my partner this year?
2. Do I feel I took good care of my partner?

3. Was I satisfied with our social life?
4. Are our finances in good shape or are they a source of worry?
5. Do most of our problems get resolved?
6. Have we found the right balance of work and play in our relationship?
7. Do we talk enough?
8. Do I feel there is enough intimacy between us?

Now take turns reading your answers to each question to your partner. Listen closely and acknowledge the facts and feelings that are revealed, but do not judge them, comment on them, or try to defend your opinions. When you have finished all the questions, make an evaluation together. Have needs gone unmet this past year? If so, make a plan to fulfill them. Are some areas of your relationship working well? Good—make a commitment to continued success.

Leave room at the end of the session to ask each other if anything has been left out. Is there a problem in the relationship that did not come out through any of the questions? Is there an area of happiness that has not been named? When you are done, end the session by stating one special characteristic you especially love about each other. Then put the notebooks away until next year and try your best to live according to the intimacies you have discovered. Make a date for another relationship review at the same time next year.

SAYING "I DO" ALL OVER AGAIN

It's becoming increasingly popular for couples who want to show a special commitment to each other to renew their vows at a second wedding ceremony. Many decide to do this at their twenty-fifth or fiftieth anniversary celebrations, but if the idea appeals to you and you're not going to hit any of those special numbers anytime soon, why wait? Now that you are alone together again, this can be the perfect time to recommit yourselves to each other and your marriage.

Renewing your vows can be as easy or as complex as you want to make it. Some couples throw a formal Saturday night party at a catering hall and arrange for clergy to lead a ceremony in which they renew their vows in public. Others invite only family to their living room and pledge themselves to one another in a quiet service in front of the hearth. Either way, or partway in between, a renewal of vows can be a very moving experience, not only for the couple but for the onlookers as well, as they contemplate their own marriages and the futures they face together.

Couples who come from close-knit communities might ask some of the original wedding attendants with whom they remain friends to attend them once again. Some renewing "brides" wear their original wedding gown—assuming they can still zip it! If you have a printed copy or video of your original wedding ceremony, you might use the words of the ceremony all over again. On the other hand, you might find it more significant to write a new service based on the knowledge you have gained in your years of marriage.

No matter how it is done, however, renewing your vows with your spouse will be a deeply satisfying experience, one that will set you on a steady course to face the challenges and opportunities you are sure to find in your new life as a couple.

Chapter
Two

LONG-DISTANCE PARENTING: NEW WAYS TO LOVE YOUR CHILD

You push your shopping cart into the supermarket and pick up a flyer to see what's on sale. Paper towels, asparagus, calcium-fortified orange juice. Uninspired, you flip over the flyer. Ben & Jerry's ice cream—now that's good fortune! You race for the frozen section, reaching back into its frosty depths to pull out containers of Phish Food, your child's favorite. Your fingers tingle with delight.

Ever since the age of thirteen, when a best friend announced that marshmallows and caramel in chocolate ice cream blended together into the closest thing to heaven, this has been your child's favorite flavor. You pull out three pints and flip them into your basket, then suddenly feel your fingers grow stiff around the container as something pointy pings in the pit of your stomach.

How could you have forgotten that your child is 2000 miles, five states, and two time zones away, and won't show up from swim team or soccer clinic or basketball practice at 5:30 in the afternoon, sweat-stained and hungry for this favorite treat, even though that's precisely what happened through all the years of high school? Then again your child might very well show up for an afternoon snack, but if so it won't be in your kitchen.

You pick up the ice cream and reluctantly place two containers of Phish Food back in the freezer, letting the third one drop from your frozen fingers back into your shopping cart. You are suddenly so depressed at the realization that your child won't be home this afternoon—or any one soon—that you promise to let yourself eat the entire container as soon as you get home. So much for the diet. How many incredibly difficult things can you be expected to cope with at once, for heaven's sake?

Natural Changes in the Family Matrix

When and where it finally hits us that our child has left home is a very personal matter. Just as every marriage is different, every relationship between a parent and child is unique. What makes one pair feel bonded can have no meaning to the next. Some parents find they can no longer eat together at a dining room table that now seems to have a gaping emptiness where their freshman used to sit, and instead they pull up stools to the kitchen counter. In time, this new arrangement begins to feel right. Others find a dull ache follows them down the hall whenever they pass their child's old bedroom and some trick of the light makes them wonder if someone isn't sitting at the old oak desk. No, they remember, the room is empty now. The dull ache may follow them around all afternoon, until dinnertime, that is, when it miraculously lifts. Mealtimes are so pleasant now, with no one criticizing the food.

Everyone copes differently. But what is common among all parents is that when the last child leaves home, you are destined for an overhaul of your entire identity, like it or not, and integral to this shift is the way you see yourself as a parent. You will never be the same again, and you know it.

But contrary to common wisdom, this doesn't spell the end of the relationship with your child. Not at all. The needy adolescent you installed in the dorm room just weeks ago didn't morph into an independent, capable adult the minute you drove off. Indeed, adulthood is still a long way off. And thus your job, which seemed as if it would change so much now that your child has left home, has not changed nearly as much as you might think. It is still as important as ever to love your child, and to show that love profusely, though now you have to do it long-distance.

Keeping in Touch Through Cyberspace

Forget your dog; forget your diamonds. Your computer is your new best friend. If you don't have one, buy one now. Today! You don't even have to go to a store. You can order on the phone from an ad in the newspaper and find the new machine camped on your doorstep three days later. If you already have a computer and use it only for word processing, sign up with an online server as soon as you can. Free disks are available at video stores and large chain stores, and most services will give you a free six-month trial.

If you are already wired, good for you! You have taken the first crucial step in staying in touch with your child. Thousands of miles may separate you, but instant contact is at your fingertips. Unlike talking on the telephone, e-mails do not require both parties to be present at the same time, a situation that is often difficult if not downright impossible to achieve between parent and college student. Another advantage to e-mailing is that emotionally difficult conversations can be dropped down to a low pitch, thus making it easier to resolve those inevitable conflicts that will arise when students get tired and cranky enough to feel criticized, parents feel neglected, or both feel misunderstood at the same time.

A child who wants to bring home a roommate for Thanksgiving break, for example, when you have already invited both sets of grandparents to stay over in your small house, can be told calmly, and in a thoughtfully reasoned argument, why this simply can't happen. Carefully constructing your language before sending your e-mail will keep a defensive reaction to a minimum. Any minifits that occur as a result of your edict will abate significantly by the time they are communicated online.

Before college started, most parents and adolescents got used to interacting at a high pitch; that is, during the chaotic, emotionally trying high-school years most conversations seemed to take place in a state of frenzy. E-mail significantly reduces that fever pitch simply because no immediate response is required. Minutes, hours, even days later, when the e-mail is finally answered, the respondent will have had a chance to think things through calmly. Learning to use this method of dealing with conflict, unwittingly encouraged by e-mail, can be a growing experience for your child, one that will be quite useful in later life.

Sending instant messages, or IMs, comes closest to actually talking together because you are both online at the same time, typing out your thoughts and sending them to each other, though often at breakneck speed. While many users of instant messaging love the convenience, others find it limited and frustrating. Thoughts must be brief to fit into the allotted space, and subtleties are pretty much impossible, as words fly quickly and nuance is difficult to achieve in these circumstances. Nevertheless, with visits home or to campus few and far between and phone conversations difficult to arrange, instant messaging has become a very useful tool for keeping in touch.

Of course, students who want their parents to check their homework and term papers before submitting them can easily send long documents as attached files on the computer. Although it can be argued that this type of attention is an inappropriate holdover from high school and will almost certainly feel like a crutch sooner or later, in the first few weeks of class some students will be happy knowing that help is only a few keystrokes away.

Communicating in Real Time

Though keeping in touch by computer is vital, there is truly no substitute for hearing a voice during those times when you are concerned about your child's adjustment. In a few seconds of conversation an astute parent can determine a child's underlying emotional state, sometimes even before making cognitive recognition of the words themselves. Whole worlds of feeling can be inferred through intonation and inflection; whether a student is tired, elated, worried, excited, or troubled, it is sure to ring out loud and clear. With the help of weekly or biweekly phone dates, a caring parent will take in all the messages a child is sending, both spoken and unspoken, and come up with a way to offer a helpful response.

Most dorm room phones today have private voice mail that can be retrieved only by the student for whom it was intended, so it is no longer necessary for parents to leave cryptic messages with roommates when they call. Nevertheless, callbacks can be hard to achieve because of students' busy schedules, long hours in the library (or at the party down the hall) and the fact that parents and students often keep very different hours.

Many families have found it a good idea to arrange a phone schedule ahead of time. Planning to speak every Sunday between 6:00 and 8:00 P.M., for example, can help alleviate parents' worries that yet another night has passed without their child calling. They know they will hear on Sunday, so they don't worry the other six days.

Parents who can afford the extra monthly bill might find putting a cell phone in their child's pocket a boon to regular communications. With a cell phone on your side you can often locate a child who likes to study outdoors on the quad or even in someone else's room. In addition, with service originating from your home area, even your out-of-state call can be billed as a local call, thus cutting down significantly on phone charges. One caveat, though: Before you sign up for service, make sure the area your child is going to has enough cell towers to transmit the signal. Some companies have better coverage than others in specific areas, and some, though they won't always tell you, have none at all.

News From Home

Even students who proclaim loudly how desperate they are to get away from the small, stifling town (or huge, impersonal city) in which they live will be happy to receive news about what's going on at home after they have begun to settle into their new surroundings. To help facilitate this, consider giving your child a subscription to the local community newspaper. If you are a member of a church or synagogue, see if you can have your child's name added to the newsletter mailing list. This can help kids feel they are still part of the community.

Some families keep a running log of neighborhood happenings that might interest their child and then send it in a weekly letter. It may not seem interesting to you that your next-door neighbor's dog had puppies or that the people up the block sold their house and the new owners installed a stone elephant on the front lawn, but sending these bits of information can help your child combat homesickness even before it starts.

He or she may scoff at the news, but don't be deceived. Just as we are afraid we will be left behind in our child's headlong rush into a new life, some level of fear at being forgotten at home inhabits a corner of the mind of every college freshman. News from home, no matter how trivial, can help alleviate this anxiety and free up your child's energy for the important tasks ahead.

PARENT-TO-PARENT TIPS

As much as we are encouraged by the experts to make a concerted effort to live our own lives once our children leave for college, there are still occasions when we need to revert back to our old model of behavior and put our children first, no questions asked, for short periods of time. One of these is when a phone call comes from college and our children want to talk to us.

Experienced parents call this a DEAL situation, and the best way to handle it is to Drop Everything And Listen. If your child is like most, you won't know right away whether the call is urgent or casual, friendly or troubled. Until you find out, the best thing to do is put aside your work, your dinner plans, or your train schedule, if you possibly can, and pay attention. Unless you are about to leave for the emergency room, it is best to give your child your time right then and there. It will not only ensure that you find out the real reason for the call, but it will also make it all the more likely your child will call again when the need arises.

Your major role now is to act as a safety net for your child's first tentative steps out into the big world. Lending a sympathetic ear is an important part of parenting at this time in a child's development, and it's a part that has to be done on the child's timetable, not our own. So hold on to the flexibility you developed during your child's high school years. You will need it now to rearrange your schedule to DEAL with your child's inevitable phone calls.

Becoming a Part of Your Child's New World

Every college in the nation puts out student publications on a daily, weekly, or monthly basis or some combination of all of the above. Newspapers, magazines, newsletters, and brochures flood the student center and compete for your child's attention. Two weeks into the first semester, ask your child which ones he or she reads, and find out if you can order subscriptions to them.

Having the same paper your child reads delivered home on a regular basis will put you in touch with your child's daily world faster than anything else. For a small fee, you will see what activities are offered, where the sports teams are playing, who is performing in what show. You will find out which faculty member is making waves, which administrator is admired, which student has painted over all the one-way signs on campus and what is likely to happen to him. If an e-mail version of the publication is available, this can be a less expensive way to subscribe, although nothing feels quite as real and immediate as a paper copy in your hand.

SENDING GOOD WISHES ON SPECIAL OCCASIONS

It can be hard on parents to miss a child's birthday, especially if it is the first time he or she has been away from home on this special day. You will be happy to hear that virtually all colleges sponsor agencies that will arrange to deliver balloons, flowers, and a cake with or without all the trimmings to the designated student. Generally you will need to make the arrangements about a week ahead of time, and you can usually pay by credit card over the phone.

Check the registration packet when it first arrives to see if the school has sent you any information about who handles this sort of event. In some schools it operates through food service; in others students run the agencies themselves. In either case, packages are usually available with cakes of different sizes and flavors that you can customize, along with a variety of balloon bouquets and flower arrangements. If you are not sent a flyer about this type of service, call the school and ask about it.

If your child attends a college that does not offer this service, check online for special occasion deliveries or call information to get an 800 number through which to order. Many famous bakeries will deliver a cake to a dorm room, and flower companies all over the country do this on a regular basis.

You can also arrange delivery of one of these special items on an un-birthday or during exams, when your child may need a special boost. Any cake is likely to turn into a party, and any student is likely to be grateful for that.

Reading the same paper and learning about the school and all its inhabitants offers many opportunities to begin conversations on neutral, nonthreatening topics. It is far easier to ask children if they or any of their friends attended the lecture by the famous foreign ambassador than if they stayed out all night at the local keg party. Sometimes, by beginning the conversation on a neutral topic, you eventually learn about the others too.

Learning about your child's environment will also make you feel more comfortable when you visit the campus on parents' weekend. If you have a rudimentary idea of where the major buildings are, you will not feel quite so lost when you follow your child around on that first campus visit. By no means should you appear to know more than your child, of course, even if you do. But sounding like someone who has taken the trouble to learn something about the college will let your child know you care.

Now is also a good time to pull out the viewbook your child's college sent last year, when this particular school was still just a speck of hope in his or her heart. Read the parts that pertain to your child's interests, and don't hesitate to call the school to have more materials sent if you want to know more.

By all means put the school's website onto your favorite sites list on the computer and check it often. If the school offers a list-serve you can join to receive bulletins or to get in touch with other parents, consider subscribing to it. Information is the key to involvement. You are sure to feel less isolated if you keep closely informed about your child's school environment.

If your child is involved in sports, you may have a built-in invitation to go to both home and away games as a booster. You will not only get to see your child in person, but you will see many members of the student body and meet other parents who can become good sources of information and comfort as the semester progresses.

In addition, faculty and administrators from the college frequently attend important games, and often the informal setting of the bleachers or the playing field makes it easy to meet a dean or even the provost or the president of the college. If the need to speak about a difficult issue arises later, it will be easier to confront it if you have already met the people ahead of time. If not, it will still help you feel closer to your child in a positive, nonintrusive way if you have a visceral sense of the people who are influential in his or her life.

How to Be a Good Visitor

Although the very concept of visiting your child may seem strange—after all, just a month or two ago this same child was living in your house—there is no escaping the fact that the dorm room is now home and you will have to ask to be invited in. Thus there is a whole new protocol to learn. How you manage the interaction makes all the difference in upping or lowering the chances that you will be willingly invited back.

Three cardinal rules apply: don't visit unannounced, don't snoop in the bedroom, and don't clean up, even if that means shoving your hands in your pockets and balling them into fists. Your child is proud of this place, be it a room, a suite, a castle, or a garret. If you possibly can manage it, try to show some approval.

Few students will turn down your generous offer to stock the refrigerator at the local grocery store or replenish the drugstore supplies. But even more welcome will be an offer for lunch or dinner at a nice restaurant. Even better would be the suggestion that one or two roommates come along.

Although you may not feel you want to give up the opportunity to see your child alone, you will find that treating some of his or her friends to dinner is always worthwhile. For one thing, you get to see your child interacting with peers, and that experience can give you more information about how things are going at college than even long private conversations. Furthermore, you have virtually guaranteed that when the friends' parents come to visit, they will take your child out for a good meal, too.

CARE PACKAGES THAT SAY I LOVE YOU

Sometimes words are not enough. For those times, a package from home can tell your child everything you can't quite figure out how to say yourself. Often it's not so much what's inside as the fact that you cared enough to make it or buy it, wrap it up and send it along. Homemade brownies packed in coffee tins have traditionally gone a long way toward cheering up a student who is close to feeling overwhelmed, and store-bought cookies in a pretty box can make the day of a freshman who got lost three times on the way to gym that morning.

Besides food, which is always welcome, all students will love a new CD or two, the Sunday color comics page from the local newspaper at home, a roll of quarters for the washing machine plus a couple of plastic bags filled with premeasured laundry soap, a packet of the latest family pictures, a clipping from a favorite magazine. You can send a small assortment of different colored pens, a travel version of a favorite game, a small pumpkin on Halloween, or an Easter basket in the spring.

The idea, of course, is to express how important your child is to you, and how you wish to make his or her world a wonderful place even though you are far away. Your child will be touched, and just as important, the very act of sending love will make you feel loved too.

Chapter
Three

THE CHARMED CIRCLE
OF FRIENDSHIP

Saturday night, and you're all dressed up with someplace to go—someplace special: your own beautiful home. Check the roast, toss the salad, stir the ratatouille one last time. Finalize the place settings and fold the napkins into those little pink peaks that look so elegant on the gold-rimmed plates. It's going to be a perfect dinner party.

Not like the last one you tried, a year ago, when you got that frantic call at ten o'clock to pick up your child at the movie theater because the power went out. Or the one before when three teenagers needed a ride home, and you were the only one who could provide it. Or the year before that, when your child raced in the door with one of those gotta-solve-it-now problems the moment you were about to serve the baked Alaska.

Tonight, for the first time in what seems like a hundred years, there will be no one interrupting the flow of the evening or the chatter of good friends, no one restricting the intimacies waiting to be exchanged in the warm, homey atmosphere you create so well.

Sure, a part of you misses the excitement, the hubbub, the New Year's Eve quality your child's social life brought into the house. And not an insignificant part of you, either. But on a night like this, when your friends are coming to your house and everything is in such good order, it's easy to see that one of the happiest perks of the empty nest is the revitalization of your social life.

Saying Hello to Smaller Demands

Everyone needs friends, of course, and somehow or other everyone finds them. But during the primary child-raising years, when children are living at home, friends are most often culled from the people you see every day in the course of your ordinary activities—parents of your child's school friends, coworkers at the office, neighbors across the street—simply because it is often complicated to arrange social time and these relationships tend to occur spontaneously. How can you find a babysitter at the list minute, for example, when your best friend just asked you out to dinner? How do you handle a child who is old enough to stay alone but won't? How can you go out with a clear mind when your teenagers are home alone all evening?

All these problems can be overcome, of course, but the great majority of couples simply give in to the primacy of family demands during the child-raising years and curtail their social schedule. Yet the day comes when their last child leaves home and suddenly this deprivation is no longer necessary.

Congratulations! You have just entered a new and wonderful place, where fun is much easier to find and your new and revitalized friendships are sure to provide love, support, and adventure.

Old Friends and New Seasons

When you think back to the time before your marriage, most likely you relied on close friends for emotional support, help when you were needy, and a sense of yourself in the outside world, all the things good friends do for us. But if you are like most people, with the onset of couplehood many of you found these individual friendships tended to wither and die for lack of nurturing. Between the extra demands on your time and the extra support you were getting from the new relationship, many of these individual friendships simply seemed less satisfying. It was only natural that other couples would become your friends, and your social life revolved around going out to dinner, the theater, the beach, and even parties in pairs.

By early parenthood, though, many people once again discover the need for individual friendships. Spouses work longer hours than be-

WORDS WORTH NOTING ABOUT FRIENDSHIP

"What are the qualities of a friend? I know the feeling I have when I am with one. It is, 'I belong here.' Seeing a good friend is like going home, or like tasting my mother's cooking. I feel secure, and need not protect myself. 'Here,' I say, 'it is safe, for I am loved.' "
—*Arnold Beisser, clinical professor of psychiatry*

"You are your friends in many ways. They reflect your moods and your characteristics, your weaknesses and your strengths, and they very realistically indicate your needs, some of which you yourself may not be aware of. Looking at your friends individually and collectively, a pattern emerges, and that pattern can be a highly accurate barometer of your emotional state."
—*Jerry Gillies, workshop leader and lecturer,*
human potential movement

"Friendship thrives, like so many natural and human things, when we acknowledge its mystery and give it room in which to grow."
—*Eugene Kennedy, psychology professor*

fore to help make ends meet, and the need to confide in someone with the same concerns as you becomes strong enough to make you seek out others in your situation. Sharing worries about discipline can seem paramount when your child is getting into trouble in school every other day, and who can understand better than someone with children of the same age? When trying to juggle a job and a toddler becomes overwhelming, who can help you sort out your priorities better than another working parent?

Unfortunately, during our children's teenage years, a number of issues conspire to force us into a kind of social isolation once again. Just when we need friendship and support the most, we seem to have the least time for them; teenagers are needy in so many time-consuming ways that keeping up with their daily lives can overshadow all of our other activities. Competition for college often rears its head halfway through high school and makes rivals of former friends and acquaintances. If we are lucky we are drawn closer to our spouses, but even so, our self-esteem suffers from the loss of outside validation of our worth. Even parents who considered themselves successful in the early stages of their children's lives now sometimes find themselves utterly at a loss as to what to do, which serves to erode their self-image even further.

Once kids leave home, however, most parents inevitably find themselves interested in building a social life again. With luck there are still some friends left who came with us through the maelstrom of our lives thus far, and with determination new networks can be created to help fill the social void.

Make a List, Check It Twice

Every living thing has a life cycle, and friendships are no exception. The first step to take to rebuild your social life is to get out your address book and see how you feel about the names you find there. Don't speak to half the people anymore? Don't despair. Mentally divide the names into three lists—those you want to continue to see, those whose relationships with you need enrichment to survive, and those whom you would just as soon abandon.

Of the names in the first list, pick three and write them down. In the next month, plan to make a date with each one. If they are couple friends, promise yourself you will call to arrange a Friday or Saturday night movie or dinner date. You have time now—don't forget how you longed for this kind of freedom just months ago. Make sure you take advantage of it before you fall into the comfortable old rut of staying home simply because you failed to make any plans.

If your list contains names of friends you see individually, without your spouse or partner, check your calendar and see what free time you have that works with the kind of activities you like to do together. Do you enjoy shopping together on a Saturday afternoon? Lunch during the week? Golf on Sunday? Remember how much easier it is now, without children to chauffeur or supervise, to find time for yourself. But make sure you do it. Try not to be put off by the very natural fear of rejection.

From the list of relationships that need nurturing, select three names and write them down on another sheet of paper. When was the last time you saw each of them? What was the last activity you shared? Have you kept up phone contact since the last time you got together?

For each name, write down how you feel it would be best to approach a revived relationship. Do you have an issue to resolve first, or has the distance between you been caused only by lack of time to get together?

Remember that as your lives have changed, your friends' have changed as well. A budding relationship that never blossomed may have time to flower now, but it is also possible that you will find you have little in common with these people today. If so, don't be disappointed. Go back to your list and see whose name is next.

If you try to add old friends back into your life in this way, you will find a new social life developing in just a few months. Inviting friends to your house most often results in a return invitation, and friends increase exponentially this way, along with new interests and a new sense of self.

QUIZ: ARE YOU A GOOD FRIEND?

Being a friend and having a friend are not quite the same thing. Although there is always a lot of give and take between friends, equality in the relationship over the long run is important. Some people are good to their friends but never let their own vulnerabilities show. Others expect emotional support but are never available when they are needed.

How good a friend are you? Take the quiz and find out, then see the scoring interpretation at the end to see how you did.

1. Can you listen without being judgmental?
2. Can you tell the difference between when your friends are asking for advice and when they just want to vent to someone?
3. Do you let your friends know they are an important part of your life?
4. Are you willing to listen when your friends have problems?
5. Do you help make your friends feel their worth and value?
6. Do you let your friends help you when you need it?
7. Is the concern your friends feel for you mutual?
8. Do your friends' interests interest you?

A score of seven "yes" answers out of eight qualifies you as excellent; five out of eight means you need to put some more effort into some of those all-important friendship skills.

Saturday Night Fervor

If you think about how you made most of your friends, you will probably discover that the relationships came about on their own. Most people do what they like to do and find people along the way who share their interests.

But say you want to find new people to socialize with and don't know where to start. What would you do if you moved to a new community? Imagine you have just arrived in town and don't know a soul. Where would you find companionship? Most likely you would start at work.

Take a moment to think about you and your spouse's coworkers. Is there anyone you like to speak with on breaks or in the cafeteria? Do you ever make a special date to go out for lunch? Would you like to expand the relationship to include after-hours socializing, or create a foursome for an evening out? It's not so hard to do, if your feelings are telling you this person could be your friend.

What about clubs and sports teams? Have you always liked volleyball but never found the time to play because you were always supervising homework? Now is the time to join a regular game. With all the extra time and energy you have since your child left home, you should allow yourself a regular night out for recreation. With common interests to get you started, you will probably find people to socialize with on the team.

You get the picture. You can take bridge lessons with your spouse and find numerous couples who would love to spend a Saturday night playing cards, munching bridge mix, and exchanging neighborhood gossip. An added bonus to recreation centered around card games is that the intergenerational mix is usually high. For many reasons, our tendency is be friends with people our own age, and getting to know like-minded people of other generations is often a very rich experience.

Solace and Solitude

In the rush to explore the excitement of a newly enriched social life, however, it is important for your well-being that you not forget to embrace your original best friend—yourself. The poet May Sarton believed we only come to know the world in solitude, and she spent a lifetime writing about the adventure of delving within to learn about the world outside.

Even if we don't plan on taking an extended inner journey anytime soon, it is still important to take time out alone every day to let our thoughts come to rest. Only when we are alone and quiet can we honestly survey our state of mind and determine if we feel right about our thoughts and feelings. Those little voices that are easy to still during busy times of the day grow louder when we sit alone and listen. Do we like what we hear? Do we feel comfortable with our own thoughts? Are we compelled to get up and get busy or do we feel okay listening to our body's rhythms?

It is also vital for our well-being to make sure we treat ourselves as well as we treat the people we care about, our friends. When we are alone and quiet, does our body complain? Are we working too hard? Resting too little? Providing ourselves with the right amount of nurture?

Just as you would alert a friend to a problem if you saw one developing, you should take an informal survey of your feelings each evening and see if there are stress points that are letting you know trouble is developing. In many ways we are all masters of deception, and even though we may live in intimacy with a soulmate, we are often still able to hide from ourselves those feelings that feel threatening.

Make it a habit to be a friend to yourself and let these most private thoughts bubble up to the surface in your daily conversations with yourself. In addition to adding a measure of serenity to your life, it will also make you a more sensitive, caring friend to the people you love.

When Your Children Are Your Best Friends

For some parents, starting a social life again is especially difficult because without having realized it, they came to depend on their children for companionship and conversation. While it is wonderful to raise children whom we like so much they can also fill the role of friends, it can be particularly painful when these special people leave home and create a friendship void in our lives. The truth is they are very hard to replace with ordinary people who would be hard-pressed to understand us the way our children do.

Yet however close we are to our children, however easily they read every nuance of our conversation, their departure for college puts an end to the day-to-day contact that has nurtured us for as long as we had them as friends. When they come home for vacations, we will once again enjoy the closeness. But in the meantime, we owe it to ourselves to make contact with peers who can begin to approach the level of understanding we crave.

We need to do this for our well-being, of course, but in some ways it is even more important that we do it for our children. Otherwise our actions will not let our children know they are permitted to bond with their peers, too. Children learn through unspoken words what we believe their obligations to us to be. They may, of course, choose not to follow them, but the fact is that disobeying a parent's deep wishes is likely to cause internal strife and conflict, taking energy away from real life and using it up in inner turmoil. Our children will be happiest knowing they are permitted to embrace their new life fully, something they will know most deeply if they see us behaving in a parallel way. New friends are a big part of their new life. They must also be a big part of ours.

What's a Friend For? Just About Everything

Friends fill many roles in our lives. They help us feel connected to the outside world and to each other as human beings. They give us emotional support when we need it. They improve our self-image by showing us that we are valuable people. They can even give us better health by helping to lower our levels of stress-induced hormones that can promote disease.

Most of us need two kinds of friendships—those that give us a social life as a couple, and those that provide a social life of our own as an individual. It is the second kind of friendship, our own individual social life, that suffers the most while we are raising children. Not only do children get in the way, but often spouses do too. Possessive spouses often can't be mollified enough to enable individual friendships to continue past marriage or serious commitment, and this can cause ruptures between friends that destroy relationships. When children leave for college, and couples have more time and energy as a result, many find a way to work out these difficulties in their relationship.

Sometimes, for the first time, they are able to confront jealousy head-on and talk through irrational feelings that are preventing one spouse from maintaining an important personal friendship. Other times, the possessive spouse finds an outlet in clubs, sports, or creative endeavors that enables a reevaluation of the level of perceived threat and results in some letting go.

In the best of circumstances, marriage partners are able to strike a new balance between closeness and separateness that allows new friendships to develop. It is important to see that your marriage can only benefit from new relationships, as they bring new life, new vitality, and new horizons to your home at a time when many people fear these gifts have walked out the door with their children. In truth there is no greater joy than discovering that our capacity to love and connect has found a way to grow.

Chapter
Four

FAMILY VALUES AND HOW THEY CHANGE

The phone rings just as you step into the shower and feel the first jets of soothing heat hit your back. Six-thirty in the morning. Who would call this early if it weren't really important? You wrestle with yourself, teetering on the edge of relaxing into the warmth, when your good angel wins and out you step out into the cold, grabbing a towel and dashing across the bedroom to the jangling telephone. There you stand in a puddle listening to your sister bawling into the receiver. It's Dad again, she wails. Another fall. Can you come right away?

Of course you'll be right there. You towel dry and step into yesterday's clothes, giving them a shake first to straighten them out a little, then grab the car keys and head crosstown to your parents' apartment. You're already wondering how it happened this time, and how many more times it will happen before your parents realize they have to make some changes in the way they live. It's been clear to you for a long time that they need more care, but it's never been your place in the family to make such declarations. That's been your sister's role all along.

When you arrive, your dad is propped up on the couch with an old-fashioned icepack on the side of his head. His left leg is extended on the cushions, the right one dangling off the side, but he says that nothing hurts. You ask what happened and get a terse, capsule summary from your mom: he wanted a glass of water, it was dark, he slipped. Perhaps the kitchen floor was wet. Why? Maybe he spilled some of the water on his way back to bed.

You and your sister exchange glances. Isn't this what happened last month? You bundle him back to bed, plant your mom next to him, where she falls immediately to sleep, mop up the kitchen floor, and prepare to depart. At the top of the stairs your sister stops you. Perhaps you could get here faster next time, she suggests. You bristle. Didn't you arrive in ten minutes, for heaven's sake? It's not like you have nothing to do, you point out. But she snaps back that she lives farther away and got here faster. And what's keeping you so busy now that there are no children at home anymore?

You open your mouth to answer, then shut it just as fast. This isn't about your parents, you suddenly realize. This is about your sister and you, and the unfinished business between you. The unfinished business that has kept you from being friends for all these years.

Adult Siblings Without Rivalry

One of the wonderful gifts that life offers after children leave home is the time, peace, and renewed energy that allows you the chance to break out of fixed roles in the family—not only your immediate family but your family of origin and your extended family too.

In the best of circumstances, you find yourself able to heal old relationships you might not have had the time or the fortitude to face while your major energy was devoted to raising your children. Many parents say that they feel compelled to reach out to estranged brothers and sisters because they notice the need for family contact in a way that is much more immediate than before. The feeling that the family is getting smaller instead of larger, and the sense that time is passing and that there might not be many more opportunities to strengthen family relationships often combine to provide the push many people need to initiate this difficult move.

Changes in family dynamics are invigorating and energizing, but as all adults know they can be extremely difficult to achieve. The family matrix is a deeply entrenched system, likened to a mobile by family therapist John Bradshaw, who explains that when one part of the mobile moves, all the others move also to compensate for the change.

Thus when one member of the family decides to break out of his or her assigned role, all the other members feel the shift and make compensating movements of their own. Talk about upsetting the apple cart! It's no wonder that the person in the family with the role of making sure no one changes works very hard at keeping everything static.

Stasis is a nice concept if you like your role; most of the time, though, adults want to break out of their assigned slot and move into one that reflects the reality of their new level of growth. When this isn't permitted, tensions often mount to such a height that relations are broken off altogether.

Unfortunately, though, even if you never see these relatives, they still have an influence on your life: It takes a certain amount of energy to keep yourself separated from them, energy best spent in other areas where it can enhance your life rather than detract from it. Now, when your last child has left home and the need to connect to family is stronger than before, it might be the right time to try to heal these rifts and gain the benefits of having friendly relatives again.

But how? The roles are still set, and the rifts are still there. Nothing has changed, you argue. This is true and not true at the same time. What has changed is your ability to deal with difficult people and your maturity level. The fact is you simply can't raise children through their

FURTHER READING ABOUT FAMILY TIES

Our bonds with our brothers and sisters are among the strongest ties we will ever experience. If they are good, they nourish and support us; if they are not they tear us down with a power few other relationships can match. To improve your closeness and friendship with your siblings, or to understand why your siblings matter so much, take a look at these two outstanding books:

The Accidental Bond: The Power of Sibling Relationships, by Susan Scarf Merrell, Random House, 1985. In this powerful book you will learn how we are influenced as adults by the forces of home and culture, heritage and values—and most profoundly, our brothers and sisters.

Brothers and Sisters: How They Shape Our Lives, by Jane Mersky Leder, St. Martin's Press, 1991. A careful explanation of how the sibling connection affects us from childhood through old age, with particular emphasis on personal growth and creative development.

teens and into the college years without learning a great deal about getting along with people. So trying again to achieve something you have failed at before, namely adjusting your relationships with family members, might just be possible now.

You must also face the reality that your family needs change when your children leave home. Just as you find it necessary to reach out further to friends, reconnecting with family at this time provides a vital way in which to feel part of something larger than yourself. The support you can get from a loving extended family can't be matched by anything else. Of course, the emotional reverse is also true: Rejection by your family can hurt more than almost any other defeat. And this push and pull is often exactly what keeps us from taking the first step.

Keepers of the Kin

Psychologists recommend several steps in attempting to reunite and reconcile relationships with estranged family members. First they suggest seriously looking at the roots of rivalry and trying to understand that you are a victim of a system unwittingly imposed on you from the outside. You and your siblings have power over one another, most often in ways you did not choose. Understanding this power balance is the first step in repairing serious rifts.

What are some of the labels you were given in your childhood that have not gone away? Can you determine which ones come from the accident of birth order? Are you the oldest child, for example, and the one looked at as the most responsible? Perhaps this is a role that was foisted upon you as a child but one you no longer want. If so, can you find a way to share the burden with those around you?

Next write down a list of your resentments. Go all out here; don't hold back. If you do this in private and do not plan to share them with anyone, you are more likely to be able to be brutally honest. Be specific and name the siblings with whom you are angry or disappointed.

A good thing to remember as we make our list is that a great many sibling troubles stem from the inequality that was naturally built into our lives as children, an inequality that happily gets reduced in size as we get older, more mature, and more accomplished. The other major source of conflict comes from parents who treat us differently, favoring one or the other and thus unconsciously ranking children in value. As painful as this may be at the time, it is also a force that fades as the years pass and parents' values become less important as our own increase in power. Love shouldn't be limited, but in reality it is, and in families there is often simply not enough to go around. Those who are shortchanged will remember it forever—and blame their siblings.

As we are making our list, this is also a good time to think about the reason family matters to us. In the course of our lives, we have the opportunity to affect the lives of very few people. Our siblings are among these very few. Part of our history is their history too, and while we may never love or even like our siblings, we will be happier if we are able to come to the point where we can accept them as they are and see them as part of our shared heritage.

When you are done, put your list away for a full week to give your subconscious the chance to come up with solutions. When the week is over, take out your list and a fresh piece of paper. On the new sheet write down one sibling and one resentment you would like to overcome.

The good news is it is never too late to make friends with your siblings. Small, simple steps like inviting the family to your house for Thanksgiving instead of automatically going to your brother's can be a good first step in changing family dynamics. You may have long resented the fact that every holiday is spent at his house, but unless you have talked it over you do not know whether he was secretly longing to get rid of the burden of always being the host and didn't know how to go about it.

Most of us want very much to have good relationships with siblings. Consider contacting your sibling and saying that you want to talk. It is good to keep in mind that the power of every step you take to improve your relationship is doubled by the fact that your sibling will take a step in reaction to yours. It may be a step toward you, which increases your positive effort, or it may be a step away, which might feel like it cancels out your own work. But every effort to reach out will be rewarded, even if by no other means than that it makes your next step a bit easier. You will grow stronger from the effort, and that is a gain in itself.

Our goal in reconciling with siblings is to stop running around in emotional circles and repeating the mistakes of the past. If we do not ever achieve the love and closeness we crave, at least we will be on good terms with our siblings. Even this level of improvement in our family relationships will go a long way to help make up for some of the loss we feel in our children growing older and leaving home.

Becoming Your Parent's Parent

Dealing with parents as they age and become dependent on us is often a defining characteristic in the lives of midlife parents. Our parents' role in our lives is to be strong, able, and independent so that we can lean on them, look up to them, and learn from them. But time plays games with us, building us up and then tearing us down and flinging us to the mercy of the winds. Unless we are strong, able, and independent adults ourselves, we will be unable to meet the challenge nature throws in our lap as our parents enter the era of old age. And unless we have dealt effectively with the pain of seeing our children off to college, we will have a far greater amount of stress and anxiety over this transition.

No one wants to trade their dependent children for dependent adults. In the months following our last child's move to college, when we have finally adjusted to the quiet house and have first begun to greet the new opportunities for growth that await us, we are often hit by an increase in need from aging parents.

Suddenly we are perceived to have more time on our hands. Siblings who have done the lion's share of parental care now see us as the ones upon whom to shift the burden. The parents themselves often long to step back to the time before our children were born, when we had more hours in the day to spend on their needs. Our own sense of guilt at having given our parents a lower priority than raising our kids for all those years kicks in as well and makes us more susceptible to overdoing our solicitation now.

Perhaps you feel happy to have the time and energy now to help out with your parents' increasing needs. If so, that is wonderful. Nevertheless, their growing dependence takes some serious management ability so that your help is effective for them and does not overwhelm you as you make the transition into your new life. It is helpful to learn early on how to protect yourself from burnout while helping your parents the best way you know how.

It is also important to think about how your parents feel as they age, and how this new dependence and the new relationship with you affects their self-image. Some age gracefully, shedding the cloak of power easily; other fight every step of the way, refusing to give in to their weakening bodies. In both cases the key to helping them is to preserve their dignity at all times, letting them let go at their own pace and helping them feel independent as long as possible.

QUIZ: DO YOU NEED TO MAKE PEACE WITH YOUR PARENTS?

More than anything else, your success in coming to terms with your aging parents holds the key to enriching your life and all your other relationships. The more successful you are in accomplishing this task, the easier it will be to feel comfortable with your children leaving home and the sooner you will be able to establish other satisfying relationships. Ask yourself these six questions:

1. Do you welcome your parents into your life?
2. Do you feel you know your parents as people?
3. Do you visit your parents out of a real desire to see them and not a sense of obligation?
4. Do you and your parents hug?
5. Do you feel comfortable taking care of your parents when necessary?
6. Are you glad you have the parents you have?

If you answered "yes" to all six, you are one of the lucky few. Four "yes" answers mean you need to think about how to improve your relationship. Only two "yes" answers mean you have some work to do on your relationship with your parents.

The Paradox of Aging

The difficulty in this is that most of us are still locked in a dance of love and anger with our parents. It is only once we learn how to reduce our need for their approval that we can begin to break free and truly be ourselves. Paradoxically, many people find that their parents' aging, though always physically difficult, also creates an environment in which it is more possible to have a good relationship. Just when you think it would be hardest, it can become easier.

Why is this so? All of a sudden, the people who loomed larger than life throughout our early years and often through much of our adulthood do not look so scary anymore. To most of us this signifies a welcome shift in the balance of power. As we feel stronger it becomes easier to be giving, and as we feel more in control it is more natural to be able to afford others their way.

Now that many decisions about your parents' lives are up to you, the feeling of helpless dependency many of us carried even into adulthood begins to break up and dissipate. Finally, after all these years, it is easier to look to our own selves for answers. The big change in our lives is the improvement of our own self-image, and this is good news for everyone, because it signals new strength and energy we can use to help our parents cope with their changing lives.

BOOKS ABOUT YOUR AGING PARENTS

To understand and accept our parents as they age, it is vital that we find a way to enter a world they are unable to explain to us. These two books present intimate portraits of parents growing older and show us in great detail how we can share their joys and sorrows, their fears and failures, and help them stay connected with us along the way.

Changing Places: A Journey With My Parents Into Their Old Age, by Judy Kramer, Penguin Putnam, 2000. Join this family as it navigates through new waters in a powerful, honest, and down-to-earth story of two parents growing older and one adult child finding the resources to help them cope.

Children of a Certain Age: Adults and Their Aging Parents, by Vivian Greenberg, Lexington Books, 1994. A useful book about how to deal with the need to be a caregiver and how to understand the complexities of the relationship between aging parents and midlife children.

Toward a New Definition of Family

It is important to keep in mind that family consists of more than just children, parents, and siblings. Many of the happiest family circles are made up of collections of relatives that bear the words "twice removed" in their relations to us. Others have more commonly designated names but have simply never been on our standard family list. Of course, they can be now. You are no longer tied to your old family ways. These new people could include cousins, both close and distant, aunts and uncles and their spouses, and the most underappreciated group of relatives of all, our in-laws.

But how do we find them if we don't know who they are? One way is to do a family heritage study and make a family tree. An increasingly popular activity in recent years, this search for one's roots has taken many people to many wonderful places, both literally and figuratively. You and your spouse can work together on this, creating two trees that will give you many branches from which to leap toward new relationships.

As we find new names of family members with whom we hope to feel a kinship, it can also be fun to gather addresses and travel to distant cities to meet them in person. When we visit our children in college we will no doubt feel the pain of separation as we prepare to go; try reducing it by planning a trip to a newfound relative in a nearby city directly afterward. This will give you a new and worthwhile emotional outlet and provide you with someone to focus on at the moment of saying good-bye to your child. Opening up your world in a new area will go far in helping you cope with the discomfort of feeling your world shrink in another. You are sure to find these new relatives as curious about you as you are about them. Many satisfying, new relationships await you on this road to family discovery.

PART II

New Freedom, Fresh Joy

Chapter Five

GOLF, TENNIS, AND GRADUATE SCHOOL

The mail has arrived and in it a brochure for the new health club that opened up last month about half a mile down the highway. You've already heard about it from friends and driven past its shiny travertine facade, but now you have an invitation to visit for an open house party on Tuesday night. Bring your sweats, it says, and take a yoga class or try out a free half-hour of personal training in the weight room. You flip over the brochure to see if there is an age requirement—maybe your college freshman would like a membership for vacations and weekends home.

You drop the rest of the mail on your desk and step out of your shoes, turning pages on your calendar, checking your child's schedule. Home for one week at Thanksgiving, three at Christmas, two in March. You can't help sighing. Who knows if kids even come home over spring break anymore? You turn over the brochure and look at the cost of membership. Higher than you thought. You'd have to go at least once a week to make it worthwhile. That's not likely to happen, you think wryly, unless you're a homebody like me.

You look at the muscled bodies in the picture, firm but mature. Sort of how you'd like to look if you had the time to exercise. Not a place for teenagers, you find yourself thinking. To staid, too formal. Besides, it's addressed to homeowner. That's certainly not your kid.

You own a decent pair of sweats, you find yourself thinking. You

flip the calendar page again. You are even free Tuesday night. You pad
down to the bedroom on your bare feet. Maybe you should start
doing some crunches tonight to get in shape for the open house.
Maybe you can get those abs to line up by next Tuesday. Maybe the
personal trainer will tell you you are ready for some advanced work-
outs.

As easy as that you have slipped beyond one of the barriers holding
you back from entering your new life. Get ready to sidestep all the rest
with your healthy new mindset, the one that keeps reminding you
that now is the time to put yourself first.

The Joys of Yoga and Other Contradictions

Once your last child is happily ensconced in college, you not only
have more free time, you also have the chance to take part in an expanded range of activities. This is one of the wonderful new freedoms
that can make a big difference in your life. Early mornings no longer
require you to supervise breakfast just to make sure something—anything!—gets eaten. Dress patrol duty no longer necessitates your
standing at the door ensuring that belly buttons are covered and that
purple hair has at least been dyed an acceptable shade. So what are
you going to do with your time?

Many people sign up for exercise classes. Step, aerobic, yoga, spinning, tai chi, kick-boxing—there are new ones offered seemingly
every week, all good for you and all worth your time. The local gym
has them; so do the Y and many community houses and adult education programs in your neighborhood. Your only problem is scraping
up the tuition, fitting into acceptable garb, and tying on the latest
sneakers.

Even if you hate to exercise, there's something to be said for
spending time in a body-sculpting class that promises you results. You
can't help feeling healthier. And the boost to your energy and good
looks will help your self-confidence and make you feel more positive.
If you can, take a class three times a week. Three classes more than
triple the value of one class in getting and keeping your body toned.

If the morning isn't your best time because of low energy levels or an early work schedule, classes also abound at night, lunchtime, and on weekends. You already know that moving around in a healthy way is good for more than just your body; the endorphins released in your brain make you happier while your bending, stretching, and flailing are making you fit.

Daily exercise routines don't have to mean spending money for classes. A half-hour walk three times a week is a gift you can give yourself with no investment other than your time. And if you can call a friend to walk with you, you can enjoy social time while you enhance your health.

If walking appeals to you, consider making a date with your spouse or partner to walk a couple of evenings a week when the weather is nice. Walking is a little like sitting down together at the dinner table: there's a natural tendency to talk. But nobody's judging the cooking, and you're not taking in calories. In fact, you're expending them, and the natural stimulation of movement gets those good ideas flowing. This is a good time to solve problems together and make plans for the future, especially since those newly released chemicals are conspiring with nature to give you a subliminal boost of optimism.

Dancing Your Way to Drama

Exercise, of course, doesn't always have to be serious. Movement is wonderful for its health benefits, but when it's fun it can make your soul sing. One way into this blissful state is dancing. Not the aerobic kind, but the sort you do on a dance floor, preferably with a partner you know and love.

If you have never taken formal dance lessons, this is an activity you might consider. Take your spouse, partner, or good friend by the hand and go out the door to the nearest dance studio. Ballroom dancing is a very old activity with a brand-new spin, and couples who master the whirling, twirling, boy-and-girling movements swear they never lived before they stepped out onto the parquet together.

Variations on the theme include folk dancing, which is the perfect type of group dance to do without a partner, and square, polka, and contra dancing, to which many people go as singles and pair up on the dance floor. The bright colors, upbeat music, quick movements, and physical contact are all mood lifters that can create energy and synergy among the dancers.

If you have the opportunity, sign up for weekly lessons for at least two months at a time. It can take a lesson or two to overcome shyness and learn the path to shedding your inhibitions, and another lesson or two until your muscles start remembering the movements and the awkwardness of starting something new begins to wear off. If after four classes you still find yourself unable to follow the music, spend lesson five sitting on the side just watching. Most likely halfway through your feet will start tapping out the rhythms, and you can take that as a sure sign that you're ready to rejoin the group on the dance floor.

If you can't quite get yourself to sign up for a class without a specific goal in mind, look ahead in your social calendar and see if there's a wedding or other large, formal party coming up. If so, set aside the time and money to learn a skill you will use to impress your friends on the dance floor at the party. Guaranteed you'll enjoy it so much you'll sign up again just for the fun of it. But if for the time being the concept of fun is too alien to embrace, by all means trick your subconscious into thinking you're accomplishing something. In a lot of ways, of course, it is true that you are; but part of the fun of dancing is doing it for its own sake, just for the fun and freedom of it. Keep doing it—for any reason—and sooner or later you will be doing it for the sheer joy.

HOW TO FIND PEOPLE TO SHARE YOUR ACTIVITIES

Do you remember the old days when people sat around in the neighborhood parks and played chess on gameboards inlaid into the tops of concrete park tables? In most communities, those days— and the chessboards—are gone, and people looking for chess partners need to go the local Y to find a game. Bridge partners are easier to find, though, as duplicate bridge clubs are listed in the phone book of most cities and small towns.

The best way to join up with a sports partner is to take a few lessons and ask the pro for the names of players on your level. This works well with tennis and will also help you find a foursome for golf. For more esoteric sports, like fencing, you are most likely to be able to find a way to arrange a bout through a group class in a university physical fitness center. Your neighborhood bowling alley will have information on league activity. You need only show up at the right time with your ball and your shoes.

If you want a walking partner, one of the best ways to find one is at your local high school's track. If you prefer the street, don't discount the value of a pet. Many dog walkers whose pooches get along find that the twice-daily jaunt to the fire hydrant down the block is much more fun with a friend. Walk your dog on a busy street and watch how many people want to share the experience.

Making Time for Sports

Many people consider learning to play golf, tennis, or any other sport that takes a long time to perfect incompatible with raising children. It's hard to justify spending five hours away from the house on a Sunday morning learning the difference between a nine iron and a putter or mastering the fine art of the two-fisted backhand when the kids have waited all week for time alone with you.

Yet sports prowess is important. We might be asked to play tennis with potential business associates; we may make new friends on the links; and we might want that good old ego boost of knowing we can hit the ball farther than anyone else.

Now you have the opportunity to hire that pro and set up a regular schedule of lessons to enhance your natural talent or find a new one. Even if you never played, it's not too late to learn golf and tennis or even to take up a new sport such as kayaking, skiing, fencing, ice skating, or archery.

However, for some of us, it's not easy to make the switch from caring for our children, earning a living, and keeping the wolf from the door to spending time in play. Our society is so goal-oriented that unless an activity is "productive," we have been trained to think twice before we let ourselves take part in it. But it's not self-indulgent to spend time developing game skills. The well-known psychologist Abraham Maslow called this push to develop ourselves self-actualization and gave it a place in our hierarchy of needs. He described it as our need to live up to our fullest and unique potential. Now, after at least two decades of devotion to raising our kids and always, or at least most often, putting ourselves last, the time has come to let the good old-fashioned work ethic loosen its grip on us just a little.

After all, we believe in giving back to the community; now is the time for giving back to ourselves. It's a way of saying thank you for all the good work we have done. The parenting books all tell us we won't hear it from the kids; why not say it to ourselves by letting a little more fun into our lives?

THE THREE V'S OF SUCCESS

Three qualities factor into our choice of activities to make them more fun: variety, value, and vision. You can maximize all three by looking closely at the roles they play in making time spent in play worthwhile.

Variety: Even if you just discovered weight-lifting and are positive it's the best method of body sculpting ever, keep doing your other activities too. Try to develop a good mix of activities to keep yourself interested, and don't overdo in one area. Balance the physical with the intellectual and the spiritual and find a way to stretch but stay within your limits by always offering yourself enough choices.

Value: If you're asking yourself, "Am I having fun yet?" you probably aren't. What your spouse or best friend likes to do to optimize spare time might not fit your description of fun. So if you've been talked into doing something that's just doesn't do it for you, stop, reconsider, and change course. For an activity to be worthwhile, it has to have value to you.

Vision: Ask yourself, does this activity fit into a goal I have for myself? Will it help me develop my career, my body, my artistic ability, my circle of friends, my life skills? Most of the time the answer will be yes. We tend to gravitate toward activities that support our visions. If you find the answer is no, stop and regroup. You have more time now, but your time is still limited. Use it well and get the most out of your efforts.

Back to School Again

Education for adults is not a new concept; it dates back to the time when medieval scholars roamed from town to town conducting lectures and leading discussions among the city folk who filled the square to hear what was new in the world of ideas. Today there is a veritable feast of opportunities for grown-ups who want to go back to school.

Choices range from single classes in a community adult ed program to Ph.D. programs at major universities that can take years to complete. In between are semester-long courses, distance-learning programs, and bachelor's degrees for adults.

You may decide to sign up for a class on the spur of the moment, or perhaps you have been waiting for years for the opportunity to start a new degree. In either case, though this may not be the optimum time to fork over another tuition check, it is the perfect time to learn. Your head is clear and your calendar is empty of obligations to your children. You have a need for stimulation since your last child left home, taking along the books, lecture notes, and term papers you always looked over and worked hard to understand. Besides, you will miss your child less if you are intellectually engaged in a pursuit of your own.

Computer classes are particularly popular with the back-to-school crowd, simply because many adults don't learn all the computer skills they need in the course of their ordinary lives without specific instruction. Basic word processing is a must for anyone in school, business, or any other profession, and even for stay-at-home parents who simply want to e-mail their kids at school. More advanced skills such as website design are very useful in marketing yourself if you decide to look for a new job or reenter the job market after years of absence. The truth is there is hardly anything you can do professionally if you are not computer proficient, and keeping up with advances in technology often means taking a course.

Up-to-Date Technology

Usually the best place to find state-of-the-art computer courses is in the continuing education department of a nearby university. Computer science professors often moonlight weekends and evenings to earn extra money, and they can be the best people to teach you how to use new software because they have to stay current in this fast-changing world to teach their classes.

Other classes that fill quickly are craft courses such as quilting, stained glass, and pottery. Artists at special craft schools associated with art museums tend to teach these best and have optimum facilities at their disposal. Before signing up, look over the credentials of the teacher, check out the level of instruction, and make sure the class is well matched to your skill level.

Another extremely popular course of study is foreign language. If you plan to go to Italy next summer and start studying Italian this fall, you will ensure a far more satisfying trip. Look for classes that stress conversation rather than literature, and you will learn much more that you'll use in your travel.

Always wanted to take a cooking class but never had the time? Now is the best time there is. Chances are you can learn to make mouth-watering soufflés, succulent roasts, and tender, flaky muffins on just a few Saturday mornings. Purchase a set of whisks, tie on your apron, and get ready to enjoy your back-to-school experience.

Classes for Life

Many classes are meant to introduce students to a world of activity they can pursue independently for many years after. For example, if you take a course in creative writing, you can keep a journal on your own that might someday develop into a memoir or a collection of short stories. If you expand your horizons now, you can reap the rewards by carrying your work through into a more creative, satisfying future.

Learning new skills that can be used in the workplace can be a good investment now that you have more freedom to create the work life you want. Let's say you've always wanted to be a travel agent but haven't a clue as to how to go about it. Take a course and find out the ins and outs of running your own agency. Or find out if the medical field is right for you by taking introductory courses in physical therapy or paramedical training.

Many courses are now given online, so if what you want to study doesn't exist in your community, you can still take the course through the distance learning option of a specialized university.

A desire for serious schooling might bring you into the admissions office of your local college to finish or even start a bachelor's degree. You will find most universities offer credit for what you have learned during the years you have lived and worked; so it will not take as long to complete a degree as if you had just finished high school. And you might very well be eligible for scholarship support if you are already paying one tuition bill for your child at college.

Getting an advanced degree such as a master's or a doctorate might have been a dream you had to put away when your last child was born, but it's never too late to go back to school to start afresh. Be prepared, however, to learn that some credits you earned years ago may no longer be accepted. However disappointing this may be, remember that the years will pass regardless of how you spend them; if you want that degree, keep in mind how fulfilling it is to work toward a goal and start your coursework now. You'll thank yourself later.

Into the Woods

It is impossible to overestimate the curative power of nature on a psyche wounded by loss. When we send our last child away to college and go home to empty rooms and silent hallways, our best therapy is often to get reacquainted with the sights and sounds and smells of nature.

Establishing a relationship with the outdoors—through gardening, hiking, watching sunsets, running along the beach—will bring you back to yourself in a way that enables you to see your place in the universe. Your good spirits will return, if only for a short time, as you let sand trickle through your fingers, walk briskly through the forest, play in the snow, or photograph a lavender dawn.

Consider taking up an outdoor sport like cross-country skiing, soccer, or softball. Many communities have recreational leagues, both single-sex and coed, that play sports games on weekends. If you used to stand on the sidelines while your children flew kites, now is the time to get one of your own. If you own a small patch of land, do some gardening that's appropriate to the season. Planting bulbs in the fall gets your hands into the healthy, clean dirt and rewards you with beautiful blooms in the early spring.

If you are fortunate enough to live near a wooded area, try spending half an hour each day among the trees. Walk the trails, sit on a log and write a journal entry, feed the winter birds, gather a mound of leaves and bury your sadness in it. Your natural optimism will be restored as you reconnect with the forces that created the world. You will soon find yourself looking forward to your daily activities with new interest.

Chapter
Six

NEW OPTIONS IN TRAVEL

It is a beautiful spring day, the kind that artists like to paint after setting up their easels along the banks of rivers and in parks with lush, green lawns. You, however, are headed for your subterranean office for another day of work.

You feel the pressure just behind your eyes and you know exactly what is wrong: You have a serious case of Travel Deficiency Disorder, a syndrome afflicting millions of people each year, most of them parents struggling to meet college tuition payments.

What makes it even worse is that you know the cure. But just like patients for whom the perfect prescription drug is just too expensive, the cure to what ails you is out of reach. There's only one way over this, and you know it.

When your kids were little and Travel Deficiency Disorder struck, your family took those pseudo vacations to ski slopes and dude ranches where you fell down mountains and off horses and scared yourself half to death. You always knew in advance it wouldn't work—how could you get away from it all when you were taking it all with you?

And now, years after your last attempt at family fun at Disney World, which resulted in a seemingly permanent state of Space Mountain–induced nausea, you have all but given up. But today, on this beautiful spring morning, you feel your determination surge once again. You can do it, you tell yourself. You can come up with a way to take a trip without spending a fortune. It's only two of you at home now. Your obligations are so much smaller than they used to be. And your time is your own now. There has to be a way.

Traveling in the Off-Season

One really effective way to reduce the cost of a vacation is to take it when others can't. Think about it. All those years when your kids were living at home were years when you could travel only in July and August or during school vacations, along with the hordes of other people tied down to the same school schedules. All those great deals you had to pass up used to bother you so much so that you stockpiled a whole stack of off-season travel brochures.

Now is the time to take them out of the drawer and look them over once again. Can you get time off in September? What about June? How about January? No, January is intersession and your child will be home from college. No problem—just book another seat on the plane. A lot of great bargain vacations to warm, sunny places are available just after New Year's, when most people are happy to go home from their holiday jaunt. Want to learn to ski properly this time? January boasts bargains at both the eastern slopes and the even more majestic terrain out west.

September is off-season for European travel but a great time for Americans to go abroad. Children are back in school, hotels are less crowded, and airfares are down. And June, just before grade school lets out, is a great time to travel with a college-age child. The days are long, the rates are not yet up to their summer highs, and a little time off between second semester and a summer job can create a nice family break.

Cost-Effective Condo Vacations and More

You can keep travel costs down if you are willing to forego some of the standard pleasures like hotel and restaurant dining and cook some of your own meals in your home-away-from-home. One way to do this is to stay in an apartment instead of a motel or lodge. The upside is you get more space—usually a living room, kitchen, and one or two bedrooms. The downside is that fewer services are available; there will be no concierge in the lobby, for example, no food service, and no laundry pickup.

But if you don't mind doing some of the work yourself, you can usually extend your one-week stay to two in exchange for doing the marketing yourself and cooking in, trimming vacation costs by about 50 percent. Condo rentals abound throughout the United States, the Caribbean, and Mexico. Many are located near centers of activity and are built for families and couples on a budget.

With your kids in college and your condo boasting an extra bedroom, you might want to share the space and the cost with close friends with whom it would be fun to travel. Most condos offer maid service, so you won't have to add cleaning up after yourself to your workload.

One caveat, though: Vacation condos fill up quickly, so book early if you can. Six months in advance is not too long a lead time. Remember to ask about special packages, like ski lift tickets or golf lessons, to make your vacation even better.

If you like the outdoors and enjoy setting your own schedule, car camping might be another type of inexpensive adventure worth a try. It's far more comfortable than backpacking because you can take along as many personal comforts as your car will hold, but it is much more flexible and outdoorsy—not to mention inexpensive—than trailer camping.

Many car campers find a night or two in the woods snuggled inside a warm, roomy tent offers a nice romantic interlude in an otherwise ordinary summer. You can pitch your tent by a lake or stream and enjoy your own private swimming area. Or you can set up camp in a family campsite with communal cooking facilities and friendly neighbors. Campers tend to be people-oriented people, and you are likely to be welcomed into an evening game of cards or checkers being played under a bright gas lantern if you indicate any interest at all.

One more option for a vacation on a shoestring is to travel along the network of midpriced bed-and-breakfast inns that dot the countryside in off-the-beaten-path areas. These small inns offer personal service and cooked-to-order breakfasts for comparatively low fees.

Rooms are generally uniquely decorated, with no two the same, and often antiques lend charm to the atmosphere. You may have to share a bath, however; most country inns and guest houses operate in converted homes that were not originally built for travelers but were designed to house a family.

Monasteries, Abbeys, and Retreats

You don't have to take a religious pilgrimage to take advantage of travel bargains available to tourists who want to sample the unusual atmosphere of religious sanctuaries for a weekend getaway or a week's retreat. You don't even have to be the same religion as your host. Sanctuaries come in all kinds: from Christian and Jewish to Hindu, Sufi, and Buddhist.

Comfortable lodgings in monasteries, abbeys, and retreats are available throughout the United States and offer some of the most unusual accommodations you can find. Most include three meals a day, and guests are permitted to visit the chapels and take part in services and meditation sessions or just wander the secluded paths and take time to reflect on their future away from their busy, noisy lives.

Most religious places offering hospitality are quiet, contemplative communities that welcome guests who want to share their level of spirituality.

Accommodations range from Southern plantations and seaside estates with tropical gardens to farmhouses, barns, and simple cabins in the woods, accessible only by a swinging suspension bridge. Some have hermitages, where one person can stay alone for a contemplative weekend. Others offer dormitory space, where men and women are separated. Most have double rooms for couples. Fees are always moderate, but sometimes supplemental donations are expected. It is best to check when you make your reservations. In order to keep prices down, many sanctuaries offer work assignments on the property in exchange for part of the lodging fee.

Reservations are essential, especially for retreats, which often book groups. Calling several months ahead is not out of line, although last-minute travelers can sometimes pick up someone else's canceled reservation on a moment's notice. You can find abbeys, monasteries, and retreats to stay at through your travel agent, the Internet, or by contacting the specific religious organizations that interest you.

Lodgings From Acapulco to Zurich

People looking for a way to see a country as travelers and not tourists often find it enjoyable to stay in someone's home, where they can mix more easily with community members and see the local culture firsthand. But how do you find a place to stay in a residential area when guidebooks only tell you about hotels? You can rent a house or apartment in a residential neighborhood by swapping homes with another couple or family through one of the many vacation exchange clubs that place travelers throughout the U.S. and overseas.

Home exchange is not a new concept in travel, but it is one that has been catching on in recent years as people have become more savvy vacationers. Although a major advantage of exchanging homes is economy, people who have done it are quick to point out that comfort and convenience are two more reasons they like it. Often a car goes along with the house or apartment, making it that much easier to visit museums and other sightseeing highlights in the area.

To find a family with whom to trade homes, most people use home-swap clubs. The largest home exchange clubs are Intervac International, located in Kristianstad, Sweden, its counterpart Invervac U.S. in San Francisco, the Vacation Exchange Club, based in Hawaii, and HomeLink in Key West, Florida. All can be found on the Internet or through your public library.

Vacation exchanges are available to Americans in countries throughout the world, with England and France leading the list of most popular destinations followed closely by destinations within the U.S., where the most sought-after states are New York, California, Florida, Colorado, and Hawaii. Most exchanges tend to range in length between two and four weeks, but shorter and longer stays are also available.

Clubs charge an annual fee for membership, usually about $100, for which you get to list your home and receive the club's directories, which describe properties available for trade categorized by country and city. It is also possible to arrange a home exchange through an individual newspaper ad in the community where you would like to vacation or by placing an item in a national travel magazine.

With kids out of the picture, some people rediscover their sense of adventure and wish to travel to new and exotic places that might have been rejected out of hand at a different time of life. Swapping homes can make these travel dreams come true.

Help Yourself to a Second Honeymoon

No doubt you remember your wedding trip with a clarity reserved for very special occasions. Just about everybody does. But if you're like most people, not all your newlywed memories are idyllic. Many of us recall lost tickets, misplaced luggage, and rental cars that wouldn't start along with the bliss of togetherness discovered on a secluded beach in the Bahamas.

Now that many years of marriage and parenthood have passed and you are entering a new stage of life, the time might be right to revisit those honeymoon days and give yourself a special vacation. Just as when you were first married, you are now starting a new life together. Celebrate it with a second honeymoon. It's a great way to mark a transition, commemorate a change, and reward your achievements all at the same time.

The first step is deciding when and where to go. You might like to go back to your first honeymoon destination, whether it was a fancy resort in the Caribbean or a private cottage in the woods. It can be fun to see what has changed and what has stayed the same, all the while experiencing your former, younger selves all over again. If you decide to go back, take along your honeymoon photos to compare then and now. And, of course, take a camera to record your new adventures.

On the other hand, as second honeymooners you might like to try something entirely new, something that reflects who you are today and how you have changed. After all, you have lived most of your adult life since the wedding, become parents, and now released your children out into the world to try their own wings. You are not just the people you were with a few more years of maturity; you've come a long way and have changed in many ways.

Perhaps you would like a little more luxury than before, and an exclusive resort would start your heart racing. Or maybe you have grown more active and a ski vacation feels right. Or perhaps you have become a collector and wish to take a jaunt overseas in search of antiques of a particular period. The idea is to honor the new people you have become and mark the transition from heads of family to couple again.

If you are among the few who didn't take a honeymoon the first time around, you might enjoy indulging yourself now at one of the traditional honeymoon destinations in Hawaii, Mexico, Florida, or the Caribbean Islands. Many couples looking for luxury enjoy cruises with

TRAVELING ON BUSINESS WITH A SPOUSE

Tensions can run high in families where one parent has to travel often for work and the other parent is left at home to supervise the kids. But when the last child leaves for college, the stay-at-home parent suddenly finds a new world opening up. For not very much extra money, a second adult can hitch a ride on a business trip and enjoy a special kind of vacation.

Many business trips involve three- to four-day stints at a professional conference, usually held in a big city with lots of tourist attractions. If you drive to the site and simply double up in the hotel room, all it will cost you is meals. You then have a few days of freedom to explore a new city. If you are lucky, you will have a car. If not, pick up a detailed city map and learn to navigate on buses and subways.

You will need a certain amount of independence to carry this off, of course, since your spouse will be at work all day, and not everyone likes taking day trips by themselves. If you are one who doesn't, ask at the conference registration table if there is an official spouse program or if any other people have asked for company. Leave your name and phone number and be assertive about following up on any names you are given.

If eating alone in a restaurant bothers you, there is always room service or a sandwich in the park at lunchtime. Enjoy the opportunity to see a new place and perhaps learn a little more about your spouse's job and coworkers. You will feel refreshed when you return home, just the reward you want from a few days' vacation.

all the trimmings, which can be lovely excursions into a very pampered world.

Whatever you choose, make sure it feels like a celebration and fills a place in your heart. Don't combine it with work, even if it would mean you could go farther or travel longer. The emphasis is on you and your relationship, and you will get the most out of it if you can put the rest of the world on hold for the time you are away, just like on a real honeymoon.

When Travel Means Adventure

Perhaps in the past taking a vacation meant a two-hour drive to the country and a stay at a roadside inn. The children would head for the pool, your spouse would find a comfortable hammock, and you would revel in a good novel and a few days away from the kitchen.

No more! Today you crave adventure, daring, speed! How did this happen? It's really not so hard to understand—you're newly released from the cloak of responsibility. It takes some people longer than others to reconnect with their preparent selves, but sooner or later everything we felt we had to repress for all those years makes itself known again. For some, the first desire to rear its head is for adventure.

What to do? Plan a vacation! Find a group that's going to hike the Himalayas. Join an expedition rafting down the Colorado River through the Grand Canyon. Sign up for a steamer trip off the coast of South America. Arrange to accompany an archaeological dig in Africa. Study nature in the Galapagos Islands. Go see the National Parks in a camper. Try helicopter skiing in Alaska.

You are limited only by your courage, your imagination, and your pocketbook. It is no longer necessary to confine yourself to trips that have your children's approval. If you have always wanted to see Tibet and can endure the difficulties involved, go for it! If getting a Eurail pass and traipsing around Europe on a grand tour is your idea of heaven, why not do it?

MADE IN THE U.S.A.

Have you ever wondered how an automobile assembly line works? Do you want to know how a sawmill operates? Would you like to see how books are bound?

If so, you should consider taking a trip to one of the many manufacturing plants around the country that open up their operations to sightseers. Check with your child's college to see if there are any in the vicinity of the school; it would be fun to combine a trip with a college visit. You can also find plants that offer industrial tours on the Internet, at your public library, or through product manufacturers themselves.

It's worth using some of your travel time and energy to satisfy your curiosity about the everyday products in your life. It can enhance your understanding of mechanical processes while teaching you about the work culture in different parts of the country, which will be especially interesting if it is where your child goes to college.

Of course family vacations were fun, and you will certainly take them again when you become grandparents. But the couples or singles trips you want now offer something that looks bigger and bolder and brighter. Take advantage of this time in your life, a time between responsibilities, to enjoy exciting new experiences, learn from them, and let your spirit feel the full extent of its freedom.

VISITING YOUR KIDS

One of the most satisfying trips you can take after your kids leave home is going to see what sort of lives they have made for themselves. Parents Weekend in the fall can be fun, but truthfully it offers little more than the opportunity to see an artificially cleaned-up dorm room and an enhanced dining facility. Dropping in for an unofficial visit can let you know what you really want to find out: that your child is living in a healthful environment, that the ordinary day-to-day activities are worthwhile, and that classes are fun and fruitful.

Always check first with your child to make sure the visit is convenient, but once it is okayed enjoy the anticipation of spending time together. What you do is less important than the fact that you are there. Kids like to know they are not losing touch with home, especially during that first year away. Planned, regular visits provide the chance for hands-on parenting again, if only for a short time, and they go a long way toward making the connection real again and helping you both feel you are still important in each other's lives.

Short visits are better than long ones, as you will find your child has many interests and numerous activities scheduled for weekends and evening hours. If you are near enough to visit for lunch or dinner and then go home again on the same day, that is ideal. If your trip involves an overnight stay, try to combine your visit to your child with a trip to a nearby tourist attraction. See your child first, then go sight-seeing. It will make it easier to leave if you have something planned. And remember that it is hard for your child to say good-bye too, even if it doesn't show. Before you go, make plans to see each other again on a specific date. You can always change it, if necessary, but knowing there is a plan will make you both feel more secure while you adjust to your new way of life.

Chapter
Seven

FINDING YOUR
CREATIVE CENTER

Your friend's announcement that your community is about to start formulating plans for its own symphony orchestra has sent you running to the storage closet in the back room. You burrow into a pile of discards and toss aside your old black ski jacket, a striped scarf you started knitting about a decade ago, two old psychology textbooks from college, and a pair of gardening overalls. There, underneath a folded embroidered tablecloth, is the black leather case you are looking for, the one with the shiny brass snaps and the tiny lock you never completely closed.

Gently you pick it up by its handle. Its weight in your hand sends you right back to when you turned twelve and your aunt and uncle took you to the music store to buy you a birthday present. There, you remember as if it were just last year and not more than three decades ago, you fell in love with a luminescent red-brown violin. You ran damp fingers over the soundboard, the bridge, the fingerboard, the pegs, the scroll. The store owner seemed to be talking in a magical language about harmonics and vibrato, saltendo and pizzicato, sonority and sweetness. Your aunt nodded. Your uncle yawned. But you clutched your violin and listened to every word.

You don't remember how they pried the violin from your fingers to wrap it in brown paper and string, but finally you took it home, giving it the place of honor on your night table. The next day a tall, mysterious woman came to your house with a music stand, a metronome, and a large square book and your lessons began, taking you on a journey you hoped would never end.

But end it did, and not with a bang but a whimper, the whimper of your firstborn child many years and many sonatas later. You're not even sure when the violin slipped from its place of honor on the night table or how it found its way to the closet, but you remember sharply the stab of sadness among the prideful feelings the night you noticed that your children were making music and you were not.

Now, with the orchestra starting in your neighborhood and your last child at college, all that has a chance to change. This time, you promise yourself, you will not lose your own music. This time you will hold on to the joy with both hands.

Bringing Your Art Back Into Your Life

Trying to pick up where you left off in areas of creative development is sure to be worth the effort a thousand times over. But it is also possible it will be harder than you think to accomplish. It is difficult for all the simple reasons—finding time and materials, making space in your psyche, getting your skills up to where they were before—but the most arduous part of the experience will be facing your emotions at having allowed yourself to stop your creative endeavor in the first place.

Uncomfortable as it is to think about, you are likely to feel a certain amount of anger once you try to pry open the part of yourself you closed off, even if you did it for the best of reasons. This is no ordinary anger but an emotion made more powerful by the fact that it was hidden all these years.

Only you know the specific circumstances that forced or cajoled you to stop your artistic work. Perhaps when the children came you decided that time and resources spent on your art were wasted, or your spouse or boss or parents pressured you to stop, or all of the above. Maybe you had to move to a new neighborhood and lost the supportive community you had depended on. There are as many reasons as there are people who lost their art as they gained their maturity.

This anger, of course, has been kept at bay all these years, and will continue to stay out of your consciousness only as long as you do not attempt to go back to your art. As such it can act as a sort of lion at the gate, keeping you locked out while keeping your artistic talents imprisoned within. If you do not attempt to face down the frightening beast, you will not have to confront the fact that it was you who put it there and you who are keeping it there, separating yourself from a part of yourself you love most.

Paradoxical as this may sound, setting up the lion and the gate is often our only recourse when we find it necessary to abandon our art. But fortunately time has passed, and with it your reasons for doing so. You must be kind to yourself now to allow your art back into your life.

Try hard to see that your reason for putting it away was justified at the time. No one who ever raised a family could honestly say that this endeavor is simple, straightforward, or without sacrifices. Art is often one of the first "frivolities" to go in our search for financial stability and emotional rootedness, two vital bases for a healthy family life. Good or bad, let your feelings wash over you now; do not try to justify or refute them. Simply accept them in their entirety and let them go up in smoke, as fully experienced feelings tend to do.

Even if you fear your hand will tremble as you grasp the paintbrush or your chin will quiver as you put the saxophone to your lips, take a step back in time and reunite yourself with your wish to create your own art and beauty. Trust that you will survive the feelings, that the lion is tame, and that you have the right to express your creativity. You have nothing to lose but inhibitions you no longer need. With the change in your family you have regained your freedom and you may—and should—use it to pursue the art you love.

The Roots of Creativity and How to Nurture Them

Experts who study creative genius have isolated five personal qualities that help us to develop our creativity. These are curiosity, sensual awareness, the ability to live with ambiguity, integration of the right and left brains, and the ability to see connections between disparate objects or ideas.

The first quality, curiosity, is built into every child but almost always gets repressed before it has a chance to satisfy itself. Find an adult who doesn't remember getting into trouble for asking too many "impolite" questions and you've got someone with a severely whitewashed memory. Great minds ask confounding questions throughout their lives. Allow yourself to not only wonder why but to ask. Curiosity leads to learning, and time spent gaining new information is the most effective way to start stacking the building blocks of creative thinking.

Increased sensitivity and sensory awareness allow information about the outside world to be accumulated, processed, and assimilated into the deep well of material we use in our creative endeavors. Take time to smell not only the coffee but the wool in your jacket and the river on the other side of town. Look at the sky as though you have never seen it before. Run your fingers slowly over the steering wheel; feel the different kinds of fur on our cat's head, body, feet, and face. Stimulate your senses by eating slowly. Try new cuisines. Listen to new music. Many ideas begin in the body and come to flower when they are welcomed into our senses. Listen for them and you will hear them as they are born into your world.

Learning to live with uncertainty is the opposite of developing the control we are taught we need to gain power in the world, power that is supposed to lead us to success. Scientists and inventors especially need to allow ambiguity to invade their world. Otherwise, in the rush to fix everything that does not immediately work, we lose the opportunity to see the forces at play at the point of transition.

The keys to making discoveries can be found when the imagination is permitted to enter those unstable areas where everything is off balance. It is here that the power of creation thrives, but only if you can stand the feeling of uncertainty that accompanies it. Those of us who have internalized the world's mandate to create order and neatness often miss out on learning from the powerful potential of chaos. Art is messy; too much order simply buries the tiny lights that can lead to great ideas.

Left- and Right-Brain Integration

Most great thinkers admit there are more than a few times they have worked on a problem and failed to find a solution despite con-

WHAT THE EXPERTS SAY ABOUT CREATIVITY

"Every child is an artist. The problem is how to remain an artist after growing up."

—*Pablo Picasso*

"There is a vitality, a life force, an energy, a quickening, that is translated through you into action, and because there is only one of you in all time, this expression is unique. If you block it, it will never exist through any other medium and will be lost."

—*Martha Graham*

"The unconscious wants truth. It ceases to speak to those who want something else more than truth."

—*Adrienne Rich*

"Imagination is more important than knowledge."

—*Albert Einstein*

centrated effort. Then suddenly, turning to another task, they found their minds illuminated by the answer that had evaded them before. Why is this? Cognitive scientists explain this phenomenon by reminding us that we have two brains—a left brain, which uses step-by-step logic, and a right brain, which thinks visually and without words. Creativity experts tell us we need to use both sides of the brain to fully develop our talents.

How can we do this? A popular technique to encourage what is called whole-brain thinking uses brainstorming or mind-mapping to solve problems and help the mind learn to work as a unit. The basic idea is to allow discrete bits of information about the problem to float in a natural, disorderly fashion before our eyes. The mind will automatically start organizing the material into a network, the same as if we contemplated the structure of a tree, a rock, or a cloud by staring at it long enough to see it as system of interconnecting pathways. The mind, it is thought, is nonlinear and self-organizing, and left to its own resources will find its way to the essence of the problem, at the bottom of which lies the solution.

The last quality of creative development is the ability to see connections where none are immediately obvious. This has long been one of the defining characteristics of intelligence and is related to the ability to allow the right brain to sort through material without the left brain imposing a structure on the activity. Most formal schooling, of course, emphasizes left brain dominance and works against our developing the ability to join unrelated objects in a unique way that creates something new.

This is one of the reasons why proponents of art education fight so hard to keep their discipline in the school curriculum at every level; without it, a great deal of creative talent is in danger of being supressed out of existence. As adults, developing our creativity or even just letting it out of the box has the potential to increase not only our art skills but all forms of thinking and assimilating knowledge in our lives.

Opportunities for Creative Work

Painting, pottery, writing, music, photography—these are just a few of the many art forms through which our unique personalities seek to express themselves. While our children were small, we provided them with space and materials to try out many different kinds of art. Scissors, construction paper, and glue graced many kitchen tables, while borrowed cellos and hand-me-down cameras got passed around among the small fry. A good place to start supporting your own art development now is to check the closet in the den and the shelves in the attic and the garage. There you will see what has survived the years of parenting, which more than likely pushed our art into a corner where it was shouted at until it learned to stay there.

Perhaps you will find an easel and half a dozen tubes of unopened oils. Or twenty-five pounds of red clay in a covered bucket under the carton of potter's tools. Maybe you will be lucky enough to come across an unfinished manuscript that can now be enlivened with the wry sense of humor developed in the iron cauldron of family life. Or the string of handcrafted bells now awash in the green patina of aging copper that you so lovingly hammered into existence in the old basement studio all those years ago.

These items can be either junk or jewels, depending on whether you see opportunity in them or not. Fingers that have spent years handling paper might thrill to the cold, primal touch of clay; eyes that spend countless hours at the computer screen could easily fall in love again with tiny black notes on a musical staff.

FURTHER READING ON CREATIVITY

The many theories about what makes a person creative have led to lively discussion among psychologists, artists, teachers, parents—everyone with a stake in helping people develop their potential to the fullest. Here are some of the best and most provocative books on the subject:

The Courage to Create, by Rollo May, W. W. Norton & Co., 1975. A world-famous psychoanalyst writes about the struggle to fulfill our creative potential, the "divine madness" he insists is our way of making coherence out of conflict as we work to develop our talents.

Art and Soul: 156 Ways to Free Your Creative Spirit, by Pam Grout, Andrews McMeel, 2000. A hands-on manual to guide you to the fulfillment of your diverse creative abilities. Encouragement along with weekly projects help you ignite your powers and set you on the way to thinking and expressing your unique thoughts and turning them into art.

Writing Past Dark: Envy, Fear, Distraction and Other Dilemmas in the Writer's Life, by Bonnie Friedman, HarperCollins, 1993. Wise and heartfelt advice for anyone who has ever faced a blank piece of paper with the wish to fill it with imaginative prose.

Drawing on the Right Side of the Brain: A Course in Enhancing Creativity and Artistic Confidence, by Betty Edwards, J. P. Tarcher, Inc., 1979. A fresh approach to drawing and seeing; an outstanding application of brain research findings to creating art and a guide to deepening artistic perceptions and developing skill and talent.

Lessons as an Investment

Art can be created at home until enough confidence has been restored for you to venture out into the world of the classroom and the studio. Here is an instance where living near a college or university is a great advantage.

Writing classes taught by published authors and art studios staffed with professional models and art teachers are a real boon to those looking for ways to nurture their rebudding creative talents. If you can, take a class with someone who works in your field of interest and teaches on the side, not someone who is primarily a teacher. It is a truism about art that you learn it by doing it; years can be wasted listening to someone telling you how rather than prodding you to find the courage to try it yourself.

Of course, suspending judgment is most important when you go back to your art. You already know this, but knowing it and doing it are two different things. Do not allow your inner censor to destroy your first baby steps by telling you that your work is not good enough. Promise yourself to work at your art for at least six months before you allow yourself to comment on it. And do not share it with anyone for at least a year.

It is also important that you allow yourself a wide range of art possibilities by including crafts and nontraditional activities on your list of possible options. For example, cooking is one of the greatly underrecognized art forms in the world. If you feel most alive in the kitchen, allow yourself to experiment with stocks and sauces as if you were dabbling in watercolors and gouache. Other domestic arts like knitting and weaving can also be most satisfying. If you have a scientific bent or like to create gadgets, upgrade your view of your tinkering activities by calling them inventing.

If you enjoy music, you have many options, whether you want to pick up an instrument where you left off, begin a new one, or try to develop enough expertise to play with a chamber group or band. Private instruction can be found by asking neighbors to recommend a teacher, posting a notice in the library, or looking at ads in the local newspaper. You can get names of professionals from the music store in your neighborhood or by calling the music teacher in your local high school. Remember that if you don't succeed with an instrument, the reason is more often a teacher who does not suit your personality and learning style than a lack of musical talent. If you are attracted to music, you will be able to learn to make it.

Most creativity is best nurtured when given free reign within the comforting confines of a structure. Try to allow regular hours for your creative endeavors and permit yourself to set up a space for your tools. If you are learning photography you do not need to set up a private darkroom in your basement right at the beginning, but setting a time to use professional studio space on a regular basis will help make your creative unconscious feel freer and more secure. Remember, it has probably been years since you allowed yourself the luxury of creative time. It is likely to take your creative center time before it trusts you to let it live and breathe once again.

Learning to Say No

While you are learning to say yes to your creative instincts, you must learn to say no to the people in your life who waste your time. This can be hard to do, but without it you will not have time for what is important to you: your art.

First, you need to get rid of the nonessentials in your life. Most organized people have a to-do list; start today to compile a not-to-do list. This should include everything that needs to be done that someone else can do. People say there are three ways to get something done: do it yourself, hire someone, or forbid a teenager from doing it. Use all three possibilities!

Add to the list all the things you do to please others because you are afraid they will be upset with you if you do not do them. Feel guilty, if you must, but guard your time jealously. In the end time is the ultimate commodity, and you will need a strong sense of self to protect the hours you want to devote to your art. People will not hesitate to try to steal them from you; do not let them. Say no simply but firmly, without equivocation. Do not say you will think about doing what they want or that you might consider it. Say no right away. It is not necessary to tell them what you are doing that is so much more important than what they want. You do not have to offer excuses or explanations. You need only to develop a strong enough sense of entitlement that you find the words to disentangle yourself from obligation to them.

If at first it feels unnatural to allow yourself the time to create, structure a time each week for a date with yourself. Take a minimum of two hours and go on an outing alone. Do not allow yourself to accomplish anything; simply go somewhere you love and spend your time there. Treat yourself to another outing the following week, and the one after that. In a short time you will be surprised to find how much you like your own company, perhaps even preferring it to that of others. This is the first step toward discovering the rich inner life that is the wellspring of your creative self.

CREATIVITY EXERCISE: A LETTER FROM THE FUTURE

Sit down alone in a quiet place with two sheets of paper, one lined, the other blank. In the middle of the blank sheet draw a circle. In it put a number that is your age plus twenty. Now draw ten lines coming out of the circle as though they were spokes on a wheel. At the end of each line write a few words that describe who you will be when you reach the age in the middle of the circle. How do you look? What job do you have? How is your family constructed? What is your home like? What about your car, your friends, your talents, your accomplishments? When you have written all the descriptions, think about this person and really try to see him or her.

Now pick up the other sheet of paper. You are going to write a letter to yourself. The letter will be from the person you have described in your circle to the person you are today. Once again, envision the person you described, the one who is twenty years older than you, and what advice he or she would give you. Think about what that person would have to say about developing your dreams and making room in your life for your creative self. What would he or she encourage you to do?

When you are done, put away the circle drawing and the letter for at least two weeks. When the time has passed, take out the letter and read it over. If it is comfortable to do so, share it with your partner or a close friend. Talk about how you might make room in your life for more of what you now know you want.

Chapter
Eight

IN SERVICE TO THE COMMUNITY

There were times last year when it seemed as though you were out at PTA meetings four evenings a week. Everyone in your family complained, but you steadfastly defended your right to go. You knew your work was valuable to the school, even if it wasn't always acknowledged. You raised funds to send needy kids on field trips. You got the school involved in the free breakfast program. You helped draft new safety rules.

Besides, attending meetings gave you the chance to learn about what was happening at school. You found out which children were winning awards, which parents were hiring tutors, which teachers could be counted on for a solid curriculum. Once you even learned about an opportunity for students to get involved in a new peer drug education program, and your child got excited and joined. It was certainly worth your time.

But when your child graduated, so did you. Regardless of your dedication, your value to the school, or your enthusiasm for the parent programs, you were out. No more socializing with other parents while you stuffed envelopes for the spring book fair or planned a debate competition.

Now as you go back to school to pick up a copy of your child's transcript for a college sports team requirement, you are greeted warmly but with a clear distance. What are you doing here? people ask, as if you no longer belong. And in fact, you are beginning to wonder your-self.

All these years you have known that your paid work was just not satisfying enough, and no matter what kind of job you held there was always something special about the volunteer work you did at school, something that brought out all the good in you. Now it's clear you need a new cause, a new place to use your energy and passion. But where do you find one?

EXERCISE: HOW TO PICK A PLACE TO VOLUNTEER

Many potential volunteers simply walk down the block to the local hospital, after-school tutoring center, or neighborhood thrift shop and ask if they can be of help. But if you want to plan your en-deavor to make sure you get the most out of your efforts, you might start by asking yourself some questions. They will help you focus your feelings and thoughts and lead you to the right volunteer op-portunity.

1. What skills can I offer?
2. What are my own needs and resources?
3. Am I a joiner or do I want to work alone?
4. What opportunities are available in my neighborhood?
5. How far am I willing to travel?
6. What skills do I want to learn?
7. What industries do I want to contribute to?
8. Is there a specific problem in society that I want to help solve?
9. What population group do I want to serve?
10. Is there a specific charity or foundation that I want to serve?
11. How much time can I commit to volunteering?

Once you have finished, look over your answers and see if you discern a pattern, then check the categories outlined earlier in this chapter to see where they point you.

A Hundred Ways to Heal the World

When your children leave home, the world shrinks in some ways but grows larger in others. Community involvement is one of the areas of your life that has a chance to grow and flower now. The potential rewards are immense: You can learn new skills, create and deepen friendships, develop networking savvy, and contribute to the happiness of scores of people. And that is just the beginning. In the best of circumstances, you can grow as a person in ways that were not available to you before, when your focus was your family and your energies were devoted to making your child's world a better place.

Many parents who are professionals find it satisfying to regularly donate a certain amount of their time to people who cannot afford to pay for their services. Attorneys volunteer to counsel elderly people in legal matters; dentists travel in groups to underdeveloped countries to provide dental care to indigent people; teachers spend part of their weekend helping kids learn basic skills in underprivileged neighborhoods.

Although you may be saddled with heavy tuition bills while your child is in college, you should not feel obligated to use all the extra time you have gained to simply work longer hours. Happiness comes from finding the right balance of many factors in your life. Too much work time can bring in dollars but keep away a sense of fulfillment, the psychic income we derive from doing something we know is important. Spending our time at an activity that makes us feel good about ourselves can recharge our batteries and make us more productive when we do go back to our jobs.

Over eighty million people in the United States spend some time each week volunteering, most of them trying to make a difference in someone's life. Some volunteer through organizations, many work on individually negotiated projects. Together they accomplish a wide range of tasks for thousands of nonprofit groups. So many people find this a worthwhile activity that there are magazines on your library's shelves devoted exclusively to volunteerism and websites that detail opportunities in every part of the country and all areas of social need.

You can pore over manuals and send away for materials from national organizations to find out exactly what kind of volunteer job is right for you. Taking this global perspective in finding volunteer opportunities may be right for you, or perhaps you simply feel a need to help a small group in your neighborhood. In either case, you will find more opportunities than you are likely to be able to handle in a lifetime. But as you consider where to put your energies, it is a good idea to look over some of the gains you can achieve from volunteering and see how to apply them to your specific goals. From there a specific volunteer plan will emerge.

A Place for Problem-Solvers

People who hold deep-seated beliefs about the way things should be often feel sure they can improve society if they can just get the chance to effect political or social change. Because it is very difficult to achieve this professionally and earn a living at the same time, most change-the-world types do so through volunteering.

Working for a political candidate in your local area is a good place to start. Government officials are always in need of help. You can donate a few hours a week to assisting in the office or work from home drafting speeches or tabulating lists of potential supporters. Fundraising skills are especially valued. If you know how to write pitch letters, or even if you are just good at stuffing and stamping envelopes, your time will be welcome. A willingness to go door-to-door to help sing the praises of a political candidate would also be very useful.

Some people with particularly strong leadership skills might want to use their abilities by becoming elected officials at the grassroots level of government. These unpaid positions as village mayor, town supervisor, or member of the board of trustees can be life-changing experiences. Volunteering to lead or participate in a community's governing board takes a lot of self-confidence; if you don't have it when you are elected, you will certainly have it by the time you finish your term.

You will gain worthwhile experience in negotiating, working on teams, making tough decisions, and standing up to the press. Your people skills will increase dramatically as you learn to deal with neighbors and residents from a position of power. And your management and organizational talents will benefit too.

Political activism on a state or national scale can also provide very exciting volunteer time. Fighting for a cause that affects millions of people or supporting a candidate whose actions can have international consequences will keep you contentedly involved in world events.

When You Want to Return the Favor

Both boys and girls who were helped by special programs while they were growing up often feel the desire to reach out to needy kids when they become adults and have the resources to help someone as they were helped.

Perhaps when you were young a Little League coach who believed in you made all the difference in developing both your soccer skills and your self-confidence. Or a scout leader offered you help, encouragement, and opportunities to shine in areas where you had failed before. Now you feel the need to give something back.

In just a few hours a week, you can learn how to coach a team of kids in a game you play well or one you are willing to learn. Even if you are lacking in athletic skill, you can help train talented athletes to use their abilities if you understand what needs to be done and can explain how to do it. You do not need to be able to play a sport well to know what it takes to do so. But you do need to be able to communicate to players what skills they need and how to acquire them.

You can also be useful to sports organizations if you are able to provide support services, such as organizing trips, driving the bus to games in another town, raising funds to purchase uniforms, cheering for your team, taking charge of food supplies, or keeping track of equipment. If you run a business or work for a sports-related company, you will be particularly useful to your group.

Scouting is still a very popular activity with today's youths, and if you have good memories from your childhood scouting experiences you will greatly enjoy offering your time and expertise to the neighborhood scout group. You will be surprised at how much scouting has been modernized and also at how much remains the same. Your scout group members will surely enjoy hearing stories about your own experiences as a child, especially if you have pictures of yourself in uniform to share.

If group leadership doesn't appeal to you, but you still want to be involved in scouting, you can volunteer your services on an administrative level. All large nonprofit organizations depend on volunteers to help run the groups on local, regional, and national levels. Start at your local scout office and see how you can be useful. Most likely you will be given a range of responsibilities from which to choose. You can plan and supervise trips or purchase and organize materials for a craft project. You can write a play for the group to direct and produce or help them gather favorite recipes to put into a youth cookbook. You can teach computer skills and direct the building of a website.

Reminiscences of happy times spent in youth groups run by religious organizations also color the memories of many successful people today. If you are one of them, consider passing on your good experiences to some of today's kids. With working parents running hither and yon to make ends meet in their increasingly stressful lives, more kids than ever rely on outside groups to provide some of the fun and nurturing the last generation of kids generally got at home. Synagogue and church youth groups often step into the breach and provide sports, art, trips and socializing for member children.

One-on-One Contact

Those who have a soft spot in their heart for the disadvantaged will find a vast choice of volunteer work suitable to their goal of helping people who need it most. Young people who live in impoverished areas or whose family life is not as stable as they would like are always in need of a helping hand. The same is true for older adults who have difficulty coping with the simplest chores of everyday life but can't afford the help they need.

If you would like to put your energies here, consider working as a tutor in a homework center. Special academic skills are not necessarily needed to help children learn. Often what they need most is someone to sit by their side and talk them through their lessons. If you can offer encouragement, if you have patience and want to make a child's school experience better, you can be helpful here.

Most town libraries have homework centers where children can go after school to work on their assignments, and many need capable adults to work one-on-one with elementary, middle, and high school students. If you have special knowledge in chemistry, say, or calculus, your work can be particularly valuable, and if you have been professionally trained to work with learning-disabled children, you will be much in demand.

But even if you just had a basic education, you can help kids organize their work and see them through it. Often special relationships develop between students and tutors when help is offered on a regular basis throughout the school year.

Adults sometimes need help with learning too. A national network of literacy volunteers trains people to work individually with those who never properly learned to read. This is a step-by-step process that you can offer in your community once you have finished learning it yourself.

Hospital volunteers do a variety of person-to-person tasks, from wheeling book carts to patients' rooms to delivering flowers and providing company for lonely patients. Those who volunteer for these activities find out very quickly how important they are by the hearty greetings they receive.

For those who like freedom of movement but still want to find a way to help, arranging to deliver Meals on Wheels a few times a week can be an excellent volunteer choice. Elderly people with limited mobility and those who are completely confined to their homes are greatly helped by this volunteer effort, and you will be part of a well-respected network of caregivers whose work is vital in helping many people make it through the day.

A Stepping-Stone to Career Success

Not all volunteer work is done for altruistic reasons. You might, for example, want to develop specific career skills that you can use to find a better job or gain a promotion and put in some volunteer hours learning that skill. At the same time, of course, you will be helping others, so even if that is not your primary goal there will still be a public benefit to your work.

Consider, for example, that you want to work on developing your speaking skills. A very good way to do this and help a nonprofit organization at the same time is to become a tour guide at a museum. If you want to learn computer skills, you might volunteer to work in a large hospital office on your day off once a week. Working your way up to a board of trustees position in a national organization like the scouts can give you credentials for moving into a paid management position later on.

Perhaps you want to become a photographer but do not have the credits to apply for a job. You could volunteer to take pictures at a ribbon-cutting ceremony for the new lion house at the local zoo and give the photos to the local newspaper fully captioned. If you ask you will probably get a photo credit, which can then go on your resume to help you find paid employment in this field.

QUIZ: DO PEOPLE SEE YOU THE WAY YOU ARE?

Imagine this dream: It is a lovely spring day and you walk past a popular restaurant on your way home from work. The doors and windows are wide open and you hear a tribute being given inside. It sounds like a wonderful person is being honored, someone who is beloved in the community because of many hours spent tutoring, mentoring, and coaching.

You are drawn inside, where you seem to recognize many faces. But you are asleep and dreaming and though you can see them clearly, they cannot see you. As you listen, the person being honored sounds more and more familiar. Suddenly you realize they are talking about you, and everything they are saying is complimentary.

Hours later you awaken, feeling unusually refreshed and happy with the day that is about to begin. You remember having had a pleasant dream, but you don't know what it was. That's okay with you; you know that dreams don't really matter.

Or do they? If you had a similar dream, would your friends and family have so many good things to say about you? Take this quiz and find out. Give yourself one point for every "yes" answer, then check at the end to see what your score means.

1. Do you pay attention to changes in your community?
2. Are you aware of social needs among those less fortunate than you?
3. Do you contribute to local political campaigns?
4. Are you involved in the economic life of your town?
5. Do you support the school system?
6. Do you work on specific causes like AIDS or homelessness?
7. Do you take part in recycling drives or recycle at home?

8. Do you donate your professional expertise to those who can't afford it?
9. Have you ever helped raise money for a local charity?
10. Do you contribute to hospital and museum fund drives?

A score of eight points means you are an exemplary citizen. Five to six points is average but still very useful. Four points or below means you should consider increasing your level of community involvement.

When It's Your Nature to Nurture

Sure, your children are off to college and all the magazines tell you your prime parenting years are over. That's all well and good, but it doesn't necessarily follow that your need to take care of kids is over too. Your arms may be empty, but your heart is full and, fortunately, so is your energy bank. This is a dynamite combination, and there are many ways to put it to good use. In fact, if word gets out in your community that you are available, you will have more offers than you can handle. This is wonderful news; it not only provides you with meaningful choices about how to use your time well, it also goes a long way toward restoring any sense of self-worth you may have lost when you left your child at college.

In today's society one of the great unfilled needs is for day-care workers. Parents are working and schools can provide just so much supervision, especially when children as young as six months old are routinely cared for outside the home. If you can spare even half a day to volunteer with young children—either after school hours or during the school day for the infant, toddler, and preschool set—you will make a huge difference in the emotional health and happiness of some of these kids.

In just a couple of hours a week you can give a great deal to a lonely child by providing a big sister or big brother relationship through a network of national organizations. If you miss your own child, you will find this volunteer work keeps your sense of self-worth alive while you make a difference in another child's life at the same time.

Don't forget that older people need companionship too. Volunteering at your local senior citizens center can be a big help in the daily routine of overloaded staff workers and provide you with the potential for warm and close relationships with the seniors themselves. You will be helping an often neglected portion of the population by providing stimulation that can improve their health and their outlook, and the knowledge that your personal touch makes a difference will make you a happier person too.

Helping Your Child's College Reach Its Goals

If after all these years of school involvement you still want more, there are many ways in which you can be useful. Volunteer to fundraise for your child's college. There are never enough dollars to fund all the activities a college wants to offer, and you will be doing a great service to the school. This is an activity that involves mostly phone calls and will not necessarily call for a campus visit. But it will put you in close touch with other parents and will help you feel you are still an important part of your child's life.

Once you know the school well, you can volunteer to join the development office's parents' committee and help to recruit prospective students by talking to high-school kids and their parents about the value of the education there. You might also consider doing fund-raising for your own alma mater. Your work on their behalf will be most appreciated, and this activity is sure to put you back in touch with some of the students and professors you knew all those years ago.

PART III

More Power
on the Job

Chapter
Nine

THE CAREER YOU
ALWAYS WANTED

I t seemed like a good idea from the moment you thought of it, spending a gorgeous fall day putting in some gardening time. The annuals were at the end of their lifetime, and though no killing frost had yet swept through your area, they were looking scraggly enough to assuage any guilt in pulling them up to plant bulbs. So out came the trowel, the kneepads, the bag of bone meal, and the sack of tulips you picked up at the flower mart last week.

You've always loved the rich black earth, ever since you were a little girl making mud pies or digging intently in the ground, convinced there was buried treasure to be found there. Now you thrill to the beauty and fragrance of your homegrown gladiolas and the carefully tended roses in your front yard. So on a warm Sunday when the brilliant sun is still scheduled to shine for a few more hours, putting in the bulbs seems like a perfect activity. The tulips and daffodils and narcissus that come up in late March and early April will be a ready reward, for sure, but the truth is you love the planting as much as the flowering.

You remember the heady fragrance of the deep pink peonies that line the walk as you clip off their stalks now to make room to dig. They always make you daydream, spinning out the lazy summer hours into ribbons of reverie. Wouldn't it be wonderful, you find yourself thinking now, to work with flowers all year round? To have a job at a cheerful florist shop, selecting blossoms for display, making showy center-pieces for parties, stringing carnations into garlands and weaving sweetheart roses into corsages?

You are up to your elbows in mulch, but your mind won't stop. You can't help seeing yourself surrounded by greenery every day of the week. Maybe you could become a landscape designer, working with gardeners to decide where to plant shade trees, how to shape the weeping cherry, whether or not the soil here could support the line of privet hedge just dug up from that old estate near the river.

Soon the bulbs are set in their soil and you move to the raspberry bushes with your pruner in hand. As you clip off the old dead shoots you feel a sense of lightheartedness you haven't experienced in months. You remember how right after college you wanted a few months to investigate working with nature, but the job offer from your firm came right away, and you knew it wasn't wise to turn it down.

Perhaps you could consider a career change now. It might be hard financially at first, but you could make it work if you were willing to make some sacrifices. Maybe you should make some calls from the of-fice tomorrow morning, just to find out if there is something better out there for you, something, you realize now, you've wanted for a long time.

Careers Outside the Mainstream

If you got your first job the day after your finished college, chances are today you're still a person with a strong work ethic, a great deal of maturity, and a lot of drive. These are wonderful qualities, and they have served you well by moving you into a solid place in the work world and enabling you to make a nice living all these years. And that's been very important to you and your family.

But now, when new vistas are opening up to you through the change in your family role, you might want to give yourself the chance to use those qualities to help carve out a niche for yourself in an area that has special meaning to you, perhaps not the area you chose when you were a freshly minted graduate. There are ways to do it that allow you to protect your future while you experiment with new ideas. This is called recareering, and it involves taking a long look at the work

VOCATIONAL TESTING: WHEN YOU JUST AREN'T SURE

While you are considering big career changes, it can be useful to evaluate whether the work you want to do suits your innate skills. You can help find this out by consulting a vocational counselor. Professionals in this field range from low-cost advisors in college counseling offices to expensive private testing services, and both offer several different types of tests to see where you fit in the work world. These tests are designed to measure your aptitudes, abilities, interests, and personality traits in a variety of areas.

If you decide to take an inventory of interests test, you will be asked a battery of questions to determine your likes and dislikes. The counselor will be looking for patterns in your responses that indicate whether your interests fall into categories, such as art or the physical sciences. In other interests tests your responses will be compared to those of a broad range of working professionals who say they are happy with their work. If your interests correspond to theirs, the profession will be considered a good match for you.

Aptitude tests approach the problem from a different angle. Some gauge your performance on a specific task, such as teaching or bookkeeping. Others begin at the opposite pole and measure the verbal or spatial skills you demonstrate, then pair them up with a profession. Still others look at how adept you are at problem solving or applying your professional judgment.

Personality tests ask questions whose answers are designed to reveal your attitudes and needs. They will attempt to determine whether or not you are outgoing, how well you work with people, and what sort of decision-making mode you use, for example. Once your personality profile is tabulated, it will be matched with a variety of professions, and an occupational prediction will be made.

For people who are talented in several areas, testing can be particularly useful in helping to set a direction. The important thing to remember is that there is no answer that is necessarily right throughout your entire career. As time passes and families change, so do our interests. It is one of the most satisfying of all possible activities to seek new work when our children go off to make lives for themselves.

world outside the one you know and finding your new place in it. The first thing to do is to acknowledge that there are alternatives, and that now is a good time to find out if there is one that suits you.

Many creative and unconventional people discover at midlife that they could only fit themselves into a mold for a limited amount of time. Sooner or later their nonconformist selves were destined to pop up and remind them of their real priorities. For example, if you've always been creative and artistic but were boxed into a repetitive job in the business world, you may have occasionally felt you were about to burst with the need for self-expression. Do you now find this feeling occurring more and more often?

If what you really like to do is to solve problems by creating new products and processes but your work entails keeping track of inventory in a set, routine way, it seems as if you are mismatched for your job. What can you do about it? Take a good long look at your interests and skills. Sit down and make a list. Indicate how many of these you use on your current job. Not enough? Think about what you would like to do, if time and money were no object. Now try to put your wishes into a realistic context. Are there careers that come to mind? Do you have contacts in those fields? Would you need retraining or another degree? Would you be willing to go back to school?

Your career development is dependent on your knowing how to use your skills, and your interests will indicate the best place to use them. Together they will point you in the direction of a possible new occupation.

Exploring Creative Alternatives

Many creative people get channeled into conventional jobs by well-meaning parents and other advisors who are concerned with their future earning power. Often this works out, but sometimes the need to create becomes too strong to deny and the job ceases to be satisfying enough to fulfill your needs. Sometimes the best solution is to find a way to be more creative within the context of your chosen profession.

For example, a trained accountant who has a strong desire to write could combine these two skills by creating a publication for employees or clients of a large financial services firm. An office manager with artistic ability could become a package designer for a consumer goods corporation.

To get started learning about possibilities that might combine your skills and interests, visit your public library and look in the vocational section in the area that interests you. See what credentials are needed to break into your field. As soon as possible, develop a relationship with a mentor in your chosen field. Mentors are professionals who are ahead of you in the same career path, and they should be people you admire and want to emulate. In the best of circumstances, they can offer you wisdom, practical guidance, and contacts in the field who will help you turn your idea into reality by giving you work.

Often you can begin your new work on weekends or during vacations, which will help you get a feel for whether you really want to make the great leap out of your current job and into this new field. If your work lends itself to freelancing, as many artistic endeavors do, you can begin to work at small jobs while employed and thus minimize your risk of leaving a steady job before you are established in a new one. This way you can take your time learning the ropes and turn your new skills into full-time work when you are ready.

QUIZ: DOES YOUR PERSONALITY SUIT YOUR JOB?

Think about each of these questions and then answer yes or no. Give yourself one point for every "yes" answer. Add up your score and check the results at the end of the quiz.

1. Are you rewarded for your work through sufficient pay or personal satisfaction?
2. Do your coworkers like you?
3. Do you have the same amount of education as your peers?
4. Do you share the same values as your coworkers?
5. Do you have the chance to express yourself on the job?
6. Do your supervisors respect you?
7. Are you using your education to solve problems on the job?
8. Does your work engage your interests?
9. Does your work give you enough satisfaction?
10. When you talk about your job, are you proud of yourself?

If you scored eight points or above, you have a high job satisfaction rating. A score of five or six points means you are sometimes dissatisfied with your choice of work, but not enough to take the risk of making a major change. If you scored four points or below, you should consider training for a new career.

Moving Ahead in the Art World

It is helpful to join a support group at the beginning of your search for a new career so you do not feel isolated. It is easier to turn dreams into reality when they are shared, especially if others who are struggling with the same goals are available to you. Sharing ideas along with successes and failures can go a long way toward making you feel you are not alone. Look in the community section of your local newspaper and see if there are other people in your area working at similar endeavors. Don't hesitate to call and suggest a meeting.

If you can't find other people who are working in your field, read trade journals and newsletters that give you information and contacts. Sign up to go to conferences and attend special events given by trade groups. If you find a national association, join the local chapter and get to know the other members. Ask them questions. Perhaps these people will someday be your coworkers. Offer to work on committees, even if you do not make any money this way. The contacts will pay off in the end; people will learn to trust you, and when work comes along they will think of you first.

It is also possible you will find public support for your endeavor in your community through an arts council or foundation. Check the phone book and the local chamber of commerce to see if anything like this exists in your area. Sometimes grants are offered to help aspiring artists get on their feet, and financial assistance or studio space might be available to individuals. You can register with your state arts agency to see if they sponsor artist-in-residence programs at public schools, art schools, or university art departments. Check with your local librarian to find specific sources of public support.

Jobs With a Social Conscience

For many people, working at a job that makes the world a better place is an important priority. But often the reality of having to make a living gets in the way of doing something we believe in. Nevertheless, it is sometimes possible to shape a second career out of a desire to improve society. Working for an activist group that promotes social justice and community involvement is one way to do this.

If making a difference is important to you, you might be able to create a place for yourself in a corporation or nonprofit organization where you can achieve your goals. Perhaps you will be able to bring a stronger ethical vision into the business world or bring new ideas and openness into the not-for-profit sector. You might find a way to clean up the environment, for example, even if it is only on a local level.

Check out these organizations that are helping to promote social consciousness on a corporate level: Business for Social Responsibility, the International Society for Ecological Economics, and the Council on Economic Priorities. On a governmental level, look into the Army Corps of Environmental Engineers to see if you can play a role in their attempts at ecological restoration.

The simple fact is that our definition of success changes as we age. If you want to rebuild a career based on a humane vision, you are not alone. Integrity, fulfillment, and making a contribution are the new ingredients of what for many has become a new work ethic. It is not enough that their work earns them money to support their family; it is also vital that it improves the quality of life for others.

According to the Bureau of Labor Statistics, jobs in the environmental field are on the increase and will be for at least the next decade. Many of these opportunities lie in technology transfer, sustainable development, education, and environmental management and compliance. An environmental professional can work as a systems analyst, attorney, journalist, regulator, or corporate manager. Researchers work in the field, in laboratories and in libraries. Environmental planners are useful as municipal solid waste managers or wetlands and floodplains experts and regional water quality engineers, to cite just a few.

Jobs in the nonprofit sector include work in trade associations or religious institutions, universities, and social welfare groups like the United Way. In these areas you can make a difference by contributing your skills in many ways, including finance, fund-raising, communications, and computer applications.

Work Your Way Around the World

If you have always wanted to work overseas but couldn't do it because of family responsibilities, this is certainly the time to reconsider your priorities. A variety of professions, crafts, and trades lend themselves to traveling and working at the same time, and opportunities abound if you can be flexible. Mechanical engineers can crew on yachts. Lawyers can staff ski resorts. Bankers can turn into tour operators. Clearly you must possess a sense of adventure and the conviction that not all parts of your life must be defined by traditional standards of success.

You will, of course, need a certain amount of capital to buy tickets and obtain visas and insurance to see you through an extended trip. But perhaps even more important than your traveling fund is your attitude: You need at least as much courage as cash.

If you have family or friends overseas, they are a good resource for finding contacts that will help you obtain work. Here is a case where knowing people not in high places but in the right places is paramount. Have you met any foreign students studying in your hometown? Are there companies in your community or organizations you can contact through work that have foreign offices? Is there a Youth Hostel Association in your neighborhood? All these places will have contacts for you if you ask.

Make sure to check with the embassies or consulates of the countries you plan to visit before you go to obtain the proper work permits. If you set up employment in the U.S. ahead of time, your agency or employer will arrange this for you. Make sure everything is in order before you go. Your official status as an employee is important for your job protection and to ensure that you encounter a minimum of bureaucratic hassles once you start working.

The easiest way to work abroad is to find a job with a firm that has branches overseas, such as Virgin Records, McDonald's, or one of the big banks or brokerages, for example. Another way is to answer an ad in an overseas journal such as a British newspaper, or to write directly to organizations like hospitals, schools, and corporations to inquire about openings. You can register with a professional association and look over their job listings, or you can look online for international employment agencies, which will be glad to try to place you overseas.

Once you select your country, contact the embassy and ask if they keep any of the country's national publications in their U.S. offices. If so, check the employment opportunities sections, and consider placing your own ad saying you are an international job-seeker and want to publicize your skills.

The travel and tourism industry abroad is always in need of workers, and readers with well-developed business instincts should especially consider jobs in sales. Those who can teach English will find employment for the academic year in a wide variety of countries and cultures.

Enhancing Your Professional Image

As you begin to look for new careers and new positions within them, pay close attention to how you present yourself and whether you are up-to-date and contemporary in your skills, your knowledge of your industry and the expression of your value system. Plan your strategy in advance to present yourself with the most punch and panache when your have an initial interview and a follow-up meeting.

If you want to get hired, think about why people get promoted. There are two factors involved: who you are and how well you will fit into the organization. To a potential employer, you are the sum of your personality, work experience, skills and education. How you present these attributes is under your control. Your knowledge and ability to learn, your decision-making skills, your communication abilities and your initiative are the ingredients that go into how you will be assessed.

Since you will probably be asked about your strengths and weaknesses, you can think about this ahead of time so you can demonstrate the kind of values you know the company wants. When you talk about yourself, your belief system should reflect your attitudes toward self-reliance, integrity, and independence. Demonstrate behavior that lets potential employers know you are likeable and have a positive attitude. Companies want employees who are proactive and will help the organization grow.

Prepare yourself to show your competence for the job by being able to discuss your skill level in a variety of ways. If you have recently gone back to school for additional training, say so. If you are looking for work in an area in which you have never worked before but have many years of experience as a volunteer, think about how to make those skills transfer over most smoothly. Knowledge is the primary resource you bring along. You do not need to know everything to do the job at this point; however, you must demonstrate that you are able to learn.

Emphasize your decision-making skills along with your flexibility and adaptability. Make it known that you are not only willing to change but are able to initiate change when necessary. Demonstrate your communications skills by speaking clearly about your abilities. And always leave behind a professional resume. Make sure that everything you do and say expresses this fact: "You can count on me."

Chapter
Ten

SHIFTING GEARS
AT WORK

Your boss buzzes you, and you save the work on your computer and walk down the hall to his office, mentally ticking off the reasons he might want to see you. He liked the report you handed in on Friday. There's nothing wrong; you're sure of that. Yet you did notice he looked sort of rushed this morning, and a bit distracted too. But running a department of twelve isn't easy. You knock softly and enter.

He is seated behind the curved cherry desk, the one you've always wanted for your own office, looking starched and officious but friendly. You feel your shoulders drop half an inch. He offers you a seat and gets right to the point. He has gotten an offer from another company. It's a great job and he can't turn it down.

Your mind spins so fast it's hard to mumble how sorry you are to see him go. He says he is sorry too. But he hopes it won't be too hard to find a replacement. He pauses, and you look up. His eyes are fixed on yours. He would like to recommend you. Would you take the promotion? You would make an excellent department head, he says.

A promotion? Department head? Now? Just when all your priorities are shifting with your last child leaving for college? You feel your face begin to redden and you put all your energies into stopping it. Calmly you ask about salary, staffing, budget. You are surprised at how openly he answers you. He tells you to take a few days to think about it, to let him know by the end of the week. You stand and shake hands.

As you turn to go, you ask him how many nights a week he gets home for dinner. Two, he tells you, grinning: Saturday and Sunday.

You promise to think seriously about his offer, but you do not tell him you have been secretly thinking of working less, not more. You are flattered, of course. But the truth is you have been considering a way to restructure your job to build in more freedom. Lately you are feeling—well, trapped.

Alternative Arrangements: Making Your Job Work for You

The day our last child leaves home is the day we get yet another chance to reinvent ourselves. Just like the time of our own graduation, our child's move out of our house and into college opens up numerous new possibilities to us, many in the world of work.

Some of us want more intensity in our lives and find it by just adding more depth to the things we are already doing; others want to go off in entirely new directions. Because work is an area in which we spend a great deal of time and energy and achieve many of our professional and personal goals, feelings about changing the way we work are often the first harbingers of some deeper changes to come.

Many feel a sense of impatience—not quite burnout, if they are lucky, but more like a deep-seated restlessness replacing their usual sense of calm, and a sudden awareness of time being limited. Long-held sources of satisfaction can seem less fulfilling. Old relationships can feel too tight, too confining. With all the changes going on at home, it might very well feel right to look for more freedom on the job. But how do you find it?

This may be the time to look at new options and consider renegotiating your contract on the job. We are trained to think there is just one way to work—full-time—but the truth is there are many variations to traditional work patterns that can be successfully implemented if you know how to argue for them. For decades effective business executives, union workers, and professionals have found ways to turn full-time work into part-time opportunities, create flexible schedules, share jobs, or work a compressed work schedule. Probably the newest addition to the bank of alternative working arrangements is telecommuting, an increasingly popular to way to keep your company job, status, and salary but gain the opportunity to add more richness and freedom to your life by doing part of your job from home.

Home Sweet Office

Do you want to shorten your commute? Improve the quality of your life? Gain more family time and even increase your productivity? With the rapid expansion of technology and our sophistication in learning how to use it for our own purposes, it is easy to set up efficient offices in our homes, our hotel rooms, even our cars, and do our work from there. Clients, colleagues, and vendors never know we are not on the company's premises; from their viewpoint, anywhere we happen to be at the moment is the office.

With the right computer setup, we can link our PCs directly into office networks and participate in teleconferencing and conference calls with clients and colleagues. We can access databases and tap into research from publications all around the world. Modems, fax machines, photocopiers, and second phone lines are commonplace at home today. With up-to-date equipment and know-how you can plug in and be productive anytime you want.

Companies have found that extreme weather that might have paralyzed their workforce years before by making them unable to reach the office now do not even interrupt the flow of business. Telecommuting employees simply keep up business as usual, working from home. If you want to keep your job and stay at the same company but change the way you work, telecommuting may be an answer.

Think of the time you spend on the road each day getting to and from the office. Want to use it for something else? The big pluses of work-at-home programs are more family time, more flexibility, and no traffic. For a family with no children living at home, an office in the house is a realistic alternative to putting in time on company premises every day. But although you may like the idea and feel you will be just as productive as ever, if not more so, you will still have to convince your boss before you can renegotiate your work contract. And that takes some planning.

QUIZ: IS TELECOMMUTING RIGHT FOR YOU?

Because working full-time has been the norm in the business world for so many generations, few of us are ever offered alternatives that could improve our lives by giving us more freedom. Yet once our children leave home, we are free to consider many new ways of doing our old job. Not everyone can succeed without the discipline of spending every hour of every day in the corporate office, however. Take this test to see if you have the personality and temperament to structure your own workday. Give yourself one point for every "yes" answer, then see how to rate your score below.

1. Even without the support and encouragement of coworkers, you are able to stay motivated to complete an assignment.
2. You finish every project you start, even if you lose interest partway through.
3. You like being alone.
4. When you are working on a creative assignment, it is important to you to control every aspect of it.
5. You enjoy spending time with people from many different backgrounds and professions.
6. Your coworkers are nice people, but you have never really felt close to any of them because you have always felt you are cut from a different cloth.
7. You like working on projects much more than directing people.
8. At the office you work as hard as everyone else, but you have always felt you could work harder in a different environment.
9. When you go to buy a car, you choose what you like, not what is most popular.
10. Socializing is okay, but work is really what gives you pleasure in life.
11. Even though your supervisor rewards people for being team players, you have always found it less productive to work in a group.
12. You don't seem to care as much about what others think of you as you care about what you think of yourself.

Now that you have completed the quiz, add up your yes answers. If you scored ten to twelve points, you are a perfect candidate for telecommuting, either part-time or full-time. With a seven- to nine-point score, you will probably do well. If you scored five to eight points, you should continue to work in the office but might consider a flex-time or job-sharing arrangement to give yourself a greater measure of freedom.

Working With the System So You Can Work Outside It

Let's say you decide an ideal work arrangement would let you spend three days a week in the office and two working from home. You know this breaks the mold. No one in your firm has ever asked for such a nontraditional work arrangement before, and you want to make a proposal. How do you go about it?

First, outline the ideal arrangement you are seeking and think through exactly how it will work. To get started on this task, begin by dividing up your job into its essential components and determine how much time you spend on each of them per week. Then consider which parts could be done from home and which must be done from the office. For example, how much time do you spend interfacing with other staff members? How many scheduled department meetings take place each week? How often must you get together with customers or clients face-to-face? Make notations of the number of hours these tasks take. From these you will determine how many hours and days you must work in your company's office.

Next, outline the tasks you perform alone, such as writing reports, researching market indicators, drafting mission statements, preparing spreadsheets, or drawing sketches. Most likely, most of these could be accomplished from a home office. Does your company's information system enable you to have database access from your home computer? If it currently does not, could such access be arranged? Are specific work materials readily available for use in your home office? If not, could they be purchased? Add up the number of hours you spend at these tasks.

Once your have examined all aspects of your job and determined the amount of time they each take, you should have a pretty good idea of how many days you will need to actually be physically present at your corporate desk and how many you can work from home. Plan the flow of a typical workday both at home and in the company's office to show how your responsibilities will be covered. Add up the number of days per week of each type of work and write out your request for your new work arrangement.

Getting to Yes

The next step is convincing your boss. The best way to do this is to think ahead about what objections might be raised and answer them in your own mind before your meeting. First on your boss's list will most likely be a concern about what is called line-of-sight management, or put another way, "If I can't see you, how do I know you're working?"

The way to deal with this objection is to turn it into a productivity issue. Since you know what you will be accomplishing each day you will be working from home, make a commitment to deliver each of these projects on a set schedule. Offer to rescind your new work agreement if you fail to complete the work as promised. Assure your boss that you will return to the office full-time if you do not meet these goals. State clearly that you realize your professional reputation is at stake, and that you will honor your commitments as you have always done.

It will be hard for your boss to argue with these assurances. However, if they are still met with skepticism, offer to try the arrangement for a set time, say, six months, and evaluate its effectiveness at the end of that time period. If it is then determined that it did not work, you will agree to go back to your old system.

Don't allow yourself to be dissuaded from your goal or, worse, bullied into believing you are asking for a favor; you are not—you are crafting a business deal in which both you and your employer stand to gain. You are offering your organization valuable expertise, industry knowledge, loyalty, and years of on-the-job experience. In return, you are asking for the flexibility that will help meet your personal needs. It is a solid deal for both of you.

Part-Time Possibilities

Creating a part-time work arrangement that is both professionally satisfying and financially sensible can be a major career challenge, even for people who work in companies known for their openness to contemporary work values. Yet the drive to incorporate newly discovered personal goals into one's work life can be so strong at this stage of life that it can direct a winning campaign that overcomes even the most stringent managerial objections.

Perhaps you've longed to convert a full-time job into a part-time opportunity but didn't think it was possible. That might be because you were not fully aware of all the numerous ways of working part-time. There are several creative approaches to take, depending on the industry, your specific job, and your salary and benefit requirements.

The most commonly known part-time work style, and often the only one people know about, is the simple reduced schedule. But even within this category there are several options that are worth exploring. For example, you could offer to reduce your work time from five to four days per week, or you might work five shortened days of four hours each, or perhaps two ten-hour days. All of these are standard part-time arrangements and are the ones most likely to be accepted by your company as viable options.

More controversial but also very satisfying is the innovative concept of job-sharing, in which two equally committed and experienced partners each work part-time in one full-time job. Within the framework of sharing the duties of one position, the two part-timers can divide their time in many ways. Each can work three days per week, with one day of overlap, or they can alternate weeks in the office with one week on and one week off. Some teams of part-timers divide the week exactly down the middle and each works two and a half days. Others find a three-day/two-day split most effective.

Job-sharing is not as prevalent as standard part-time work and is still considered to be in the experimental stage, but it is part of the mainstream in many forward-thinking corporations and is gaining in popularity each year.

Options for Professionals

The third type of part-time work is achieved by signing up with a temporary agency in your professional field and working at jobs assigned to you through them. For this service you will be required to pay a fee. Usually a portion of your paycheck issued through the agency will be withheld as payment. Part-time temp work is available to a broad range of professionals, including physicians, accountants, engineers, writers, computer programmers, insurance experts, marketing specialists, and management executives.

If you choose to work part-time or work out a job-sharing arrangement with a coworker, some of your benefits will continue but others will not. Those that are statutory, or required by law, cannot be taken away from you. These include Social Security liability and pay for unemployment insurance premiums, which are yours regardless of the hours you work. In addition, companies that offer a 401(k) retirement plan for full-time employees must also do so for those who work part-time.

Outside of these requirements, however, companies are on their own in determining what to give you. Some prorate your old benefits based on the number of hours you will work part-time; others offer little or no medical coverage, insurance, or vacation time. The fact is virtually all benefits need to be individually negotiated.

Coming to terms with the trade-offs you must make to work part-time is no easy task. It helps to have a clear perspective by writing down what you value most. List your priorities—such as job status, income, flexibility, family time, long-term financial security—and then order them. Then look realistically at your resources and sources of support other than your job. While you are working this out, keep in mind that choosing to go part-time now need not be a permanent commitment. If it doesn't work out as well as you had hoped, there is always the chance to change it back.

RESOURCES FOR ALTERNATIVE WORK STYLES

Every worker knows that making a living and creating a life are not necessarily the same thing. The lucky ones have found ways to enjoy their work while making enough money to support their family, but many are still searching. Here are four excellent guides to changing your work style to accommodate your needs and goals.

Work a Four-Hour Day: Achieving Business Efficiency on Your Own Terms, by Arthur Robertson and William Proctor, Avon Books, 1994. Shows you how to plan your workday so that you have time left over for your other pursuits and explains how to negotiate with your boss to get the new arrangement signed, sealed, and approved.

Six Months Off: How to Plan, Negotiate and Take the Break You Need Without Burning Bridges or Going Broke, by Hope Deligozima, James Scott, and David Sharp, Henry Holt, 1996. Follow the step-by-step plan in this excellent guidebook to design a sabbatical. You will find sections on how to counter objections about time and money, how to make the most of your time, and how to return to your job refreshed and invigorated.

Working Free: Practical Alternatives to the Nine-to-Five Job, by John Applegath, Amacom, 1982. You can gain more flexibility and more autonomy at work by reorganizing what you do and how you do it. Learn from a diverse group of people who actually did it and live richer, more fulfilling lives as a result.

Working From Home: Everything You Need to Know About Living and Working Under the Same Roof, by Paul and Sarah Edwards, J. P. Tarcher, 1987. The classic guide to earning a living without leaving your house. This book shows you how to keep your job but get it done through telecommuting and also how to piece together a new work life using the power of technology coupled with your talents and determination.

How to Argue for Part-Time Work and Win

Even if you've worked for only one or two companies in your life, you probably already know how hard it is to effect change in corporate America on an individual basis. Many ideas, though old-fashioned and outdated, are so entrenched in company policies that it can feel as though you will need some form of dynamite to jolt senior management out of its set and solid ways.

But the right words can go a long way toward helping you make the case for professional part-time work, and convincing management to be flexible is largely a matter of appealing to what means the most to them. The most powerful weapon you have, the threat of leaving your job, plays right into one of their most important organizational goals: to retain experienced employees and avoid having to pay the high cost of training new ones.

As a full-timer with many years' experience, you are well qualified to help achieve your company's goals, and your leaving would create a hole in the organization. Traditional industry estimates show that it costs 150 percent of your salary to recruit, hire, and train your replacement. In addition, your company has invested quite a bit of money in salary and benefits in you. Although they may not acknowledge this, it is far more cost effective for your company to accept your plan to work part-time than to have you leave.

You might also add that your experience with the company makes you far more valuable to them than a new employee, who does not know how to deal with clients and customers the way you do. All organizations must stay competitive in the marketplace to prosper, and your knowledge and experience helps them to do so.

Forward-thinking companies will see that offering a part-time professional work option will also attract an expanded talent pool and enable them to hire people who are simply not available full-time. In addition, part-time workers are often the most productive, as they have a limited time in which to accomplish their work tasks and no time on the job for outside activities. Of all workers, they are the most likely to produce 100 percent of the time they are at work, as they have the hours on their days off to take care of personal tasks and thus will not do them on company time.

Finally, you should point out that allowing you to work part-time costs the company nothing and has the potential of giving back a lot. Overhead stays the same, as does the cost of accounting, yet the rise in employee morale is potentially high. And as every manager knows, the high spirits of one employee tend to lift the morale of the others.

Chapter
Eleven

JOBS THAT USE YOUR NURTURING SKILLS

It wasn't your idea, getting the bicycles out of storage for one more ride before winter closed in on you. Just because the cold weather was slow in coming this year didn't mean you had to listen to your neighbor's harebrained scheme to take the bikes down to the cement beach path, the one open only to pedestrians. In the off-season like this, you figured, there would be few walkers to complain about illegal bikers, and you had to admit it sounded enticing, getting one more chance to smell the salt air, listen to the gulls, and feel the warm sun on your back.

Of course, you had no way to know then how the day would turn out. It started innocently enough, with the two of you loading your ten-speeds on the top of the car, then sailing down the boardwalk on your bikes, wind blowing through your hair, lunches stashed snugly on the back fender.

It was even easy to maneuver off the boardwalk and down the walkway through the tall grasses to the beach path, where you saw no sign of any beach patrol personnel, or anyone else for that matter. Now, with the path narrow but no one else on it, there is room for the two of you to ride side by side. Even when the path slims down to single file, it is easy to slip in front and pedal steadily through the afternoon sunshine.

It is only when you round the first curve that you lose your balance for a moment, but you set the bike straight right away with nothing more than a small swerve. It is the second curve that makes you stumble and this time you go down, landing on your left elbow and hip with the bike toppling over on you. You know right away what went wrong when you see the section of cement that lies buckled under your back wheel.

Your friend helps you up and asks if you are all right, but before you can answer there is a sharp stab of pain through your elbow, and suddenly you know for sure you have broken your arm. It is hard riding your bike back to the car, feeling the numbness creep up your forearm, but you have no choice. Your friend drives you to the hospital, and before you know it you have been whisked through the emergency room and into X-ray and outfitted with a cold, wet plaster cast.

You can't remember the last time you had to fight back tears of pain, but you lose the battle handily this time. A nurse hands you tissues; another brings you a cup of tea. A third tells you to close your eyes until you feel strong enough to go on, tucking a blanket gently under your chin. You lie there, exhausted and humbled but grateful. It has been years since you felt so helpless. It has been years since you had to let strangers take care of you. It has been years since you realized how good it feels when they do.

New Directions for Work

More and more often, the careers people choose when they are just out of college are not the ones from which they retire forty or fifty years later. As our interests emerge and our families grow and develop, many of us find ourselves pursuing new opportunities that change the way we see our place in the world. Parenthood can be one of those experiences that changes the course of our careers.

Through caring for our children we sometimes discover hidden talents and passions we never knew existed in our psyches. Though we might have chosen careers in financial services or engineering design in our early twenties, by the time we are halfway through raising our children we find out how good we are at helping children learn and unraveling their emotional problems. And when those children grow up and leave home, we find ourselves drawn to new careers in teaching or therapy or nursing.

Those who found great joy in nurturing their families may find that today's empty nest demands they reach out to others in similar ways. If you are one of these people, this might be the time for you to consider a new career in a field that allows you to help others. There is a vast array of choices in the helping professions, with variations ranging from work environment, degree of financial reward, educational requirements, and level of emotional commitment. Although each profession is unique, what they all have in common is that they use the skills and talents honed in parenthood and provide the same deep type of personal satisfaction of a job well done.

When we think of nurturing careers many of us think first of the medical profession. But the helping professions also encompass day care workers, teachers, counselors and therapists, clergy, social workers, nutritionists, and psychologists, and that's just the short list.

But are jobs in these fields readily available today? Can we realistically train for new professional work of this sort in middle age? Will we be able to achieve the levels of status and income we want and need if we begin now? Let's consider some of the options.

Popular Careers in Health Care

From physicians and chiropractors to midwives and mental health experts, medical workers are among the most respected professionals in our society. Dentists and dieticians, EMTs and pharmacists all enjoy careers that require commitment, dedication, and integrity and engender respect and a deep sense of self-worth. But of all of these, when asked who provides the most effective helping hands in health care, most of us would think first of nurses.

Because of its unique place in the traditional hierarchy of the medical profession, nursing was slower than other areas in gaining the much-needed increases in status and financial rewards brought about by the women's movement. Today it has caught up and once again offers dedicated medical workers virtually unbounded opportunities as respected members of health care teams, providing for the physical, mental, and emotional care of patients.

Of the three most highly respected professional categories of nursing, registered nurses, or RNs, are the most well known. Most RNs are
employed by hospitals and are the first professionals patients see in a
health care setting. They need an abundance of both physical and
emotional stamina to handle the demands of their job, plus several
years of formal training to prepare for it.

If you are considering going back to school for a degree in nursing,
you have three options, depending on whether you want to study in a
hospital or a university. Many hospitals run their own nursing schools
and offer a three-year diploma program that combines clinical experience on the floor with classroom instruction. Or you may prefer a
four-year baccalaureate program at a university nursing school, which
would give you a bachelor of science in nursing (BSN) degree. Two-
year associate degree programs are also available at many community
colleges.

A partially or fully completed bachelor's degree earned in another
field may qualify you for credits in nursing, so that the new degree
might not take the full amount of time to achieve. In any case, you will
have to pass a national certification exam to obtain a nursing license.

If you are mainly interested in providing bedside care for patients
in nursing homes, rehabilitation centers, and hospitals, you might decide to become a licensed practical nurse, or an LPN. One-year state-
approved programs at trade or vocational schools or local hospitals
provide the education needed, and training is also available in junior
colleges and health agencies. A caring and sympathetic nature is as important as emotional stability and physical stamina for this job, and
the ability to take orders and carry them through is also necessary.
LPNs work under close supervision of physicians and RNs.

Medical professionals who want to work independently often find
their best answer is to become nurse practitioners. These health care
providers are registered nurses with advanced education and clinical
training in a specialty area, such as pediatrics, acute care, or geriatrics.
As primary caregivers, they provide medical services directly to individuals and families by diagnosing and managing illnesses and providing disease prevention services. An extra degree of professionalism is
needed here, in addition to compassion and leadership skill, because
of the additional responsibility inherent in the job. Education to be-

come a nurse practitioner includes a bachelor's degree, a master's degree, and post-master's training.

Responding to a Higher Call

Religion is more than a system of beliefs to many people; it is a career. Extrapolating the role of parent to extend beyond ministering to our own children can bring us to a new plane, one in which our ability to provide moral guidance and spiritual care benefits a wide variety of individuals and families within our faith.

Training as a clergyperson almost always involves advanced degrees for ordination. Religious leaders need to be able to minister to the whole person—mind, body, and spirit. This requires facility and knowledge in many areas: public speaking, psychology, theology, philosophy, and history, plus talent in leadership, skill in listening to people, and compassion toward humanity. Three to four years of graduate study is the norm if your goal is to become a congregational leader.

However, not every clergyperson wants to work full-time in the pulpit. Some choose to become chaplains, spiritual leaders who serve the needs of a group of people within a program or institution. For example, most hospitals employ chaplains in each of the country's major religions to lead services, minister to the private spiritual needs of patients and their families, and offer religious counseling where needed. An interest in healing and the ability to bond quickly with strangers are two special qualities that help define a successful hospital chaplain.

State and federal prisons also employ chaplains, as do local jails and county prisons, and they are also extensively used throughout the military. Additionally, chaplains run programs on college campuses, administering denominational facilities and providing centers for religious thought and practice. This job will undoubtedly have particular appeal for parents of college-age children, because of their special knowledge of the needs, fears, and goals of this age group.

It is not necessary to earn an ordination certificate or a degree in religion to teach in many private day schools or after-school or weekend programs run by synagogues and churches. Many people who no longer have children at home to parent find deep satisfaction guiding other young people through classroom instruction and youth group activities sponsored by their religious center.

Work That Makes a Difference

If your prime satisfaction in parenting was knowing you were improving the lives of your children, you might want to consider a career in counseling and human development, now that you have graduated out of your primary parenting years.

This is a field that provides you with a wide array of opportunities as a first-time job seeker and will also have much to offer when you become a seasoned professional. People in all walks of life face difficulties, want advice, and need professionals to help make their lives better. If you are good at encouraging people and helping them find solutions to personal, social, educational, and career issues in their lives, you might want to consider counseling as a profession.

Most counselors work in schools, rehabilitation centers, or mental health facilities. Their services run the gamut from helping emotionally disabled people become self-sufficient, steering students toward the right college, providing career information for clients, and suggesting specific jobs to working closely with psychiatrists and social workers in a therapy setting. Other counselors work with problems of physical abuse, parenting, retirement, bereavement, drug abuse, and family relationships.

Most counselor positions require a master's degree, and for some you will need an additional year of supervised experience. However, there are many organizations that will hire counselors for entry-level positions with only a bachelor's degree and give them a specified number of years to earn a master's part-time. In most cases, certification is required at the end of the educational period.

Enriching the Lives of Children

Some of us always knew we wanted to become parents; others only fell in love with our children once they were born. But many of us are subject to developing a kind of universal child-love that never leaves us, even after our children have grown up and left home. For those of who fall into this category, careers that entail close work with children can offer a happy alternative to work we might have chosen before we fully understood our inner nature.

Fortunately the burgeoning area of child care is open wider than ever today, with opportunities growing as the population increases and working parents require more help in ensuring the care and well-being of their kids. Entry into this field is easier than in other professions because of the wide variety of levels of training requirements and degrees of certification.

Although not highly paid, child-care careers are considered very important in our society and provide a kind of satisfaction that is matched by few other professions. Here is an opportunity to combine instinct and education, experience and theoretical knowledge, and come out with a career opportunity that is unique to your talents. Your interaction with the children in your care cannot be duplicated by anyone else, and your creative efforts to help them grow are simply not available in any other venue. And perhaps even more important, your work has results you can see: happy children, contented parents, and a stimulating, growth-oriented environment.

The employment of child-care workers is expected to grow much faster than the average for all occupations through the next decade. Most child-care workers will find jobs in day-care centers, two-thirds of which are nonprofit, run by school districts, religious institutions, and community agencies like YMCAs and parent associations. For-profit centers that are operated by regional and national chains or independent organizations comprise about 30 percent of child-care facilities. The tiny remaining balance, about 5 percent, is made up of corporations that operate centers for their employees' children.

The most rapidly growing area in the field of child care is extended-day care, in which older children are cared for after school. Most traditional child-care centers end at kindergarten age; extended-day care is designed for children in kindergarten through middle school and typically offers two to four hours of homework help after school plus arts and crafts, sports activities, music classes, and academic enrichment.

A HOME FOR EVERY CHILD

No one knows better than the parent of a college-age child how valuable it is to have a nurturing home. Through your efforts your child is now launched into the larger world, ready to take on the challenges and reap the rewards of successful choices. Wouldn't it be wonderful to help other children find homes where they can have the same chance to grow up with honor, pride, and support?

A small but growing number of empty-nest parents have put their personal and professional expertise toward a career in adoption services. Some have social work backgrounds already; others come from entirely different fields and go back to school for a master's degree and then move directly into social welfare agencies upon graduation. In smaller communities it is sometimes possible to get a job in this field with only a bachelor's degree in psychology or sociology or related work experience. Virtually all states have licensing and certification regulations regarding social work practice and the use of professional titles.

It usually takes two years to complete the classroom study and field work for a master's degree; most include about 900 hours of supervised internship work. But it is generally not a requirement for admission into the program to have a bachelor's degree in sociology. For those who do, however, many schools offer an accelerated program of study. Although the educational requirements to become a social worker are roughly equivalent to those of a teacher, the pay and benefits are both less. Entering this field takes an unusual degree of dedication in addition to emotional strength, high intelligence, and good judgment.

Professionals in adoption services work with children who are dependents of the state either because they have no parents at birth or have been taken away from their parents by the courts. Many are high-risk children who have been abandoned or abused. Often they are chronically ill or handicapped; some are both retarded and disabled. But many are perfectly healthy and have every chance to succeed in a supportive home.

As the child's guardian, the adoption professional is charged with assessing his or her adoption needs and finding a range of suitable homes. Once one is selected, he or she studies the home and family to see if it is a good match for the child. If it is, and the adoption procedure is put into place, the adoption professional coordinates all the efforts until the legal proceedings are completed.

Finally, he or she makes a genetic search for the child's natural parents so that the records are complete and the adoptee and both parents can find each other if they want to when the child reaches legal age, at nineteen.

More information on entering the expanding field of adoption services can be obtained from the Child Welfare League of America at 440 First St., N.W., Suite 310, Washington, D.C. 20001, and the National Association of Social Workers, 750 First St., N.E., Suite 700, Washington, D.C. 20002.

Workers at all levels of child care need a thorough knowledge of the stages of child development and a variety of child-rearing practices, along with highly developed nurturing skills and the ability to communicate well. Talent in music, drama, art, and storytelling can be very helpful too.

Most states today have legislation requiring child-care workers to take specific courses and programs, but few require any particular type of certification. However, a background in early childhood education and child development or certification in nursing or social work would be a useful credential. But while some formal coursework is helpful, there is as yet no standardization of requirements for either teachers or their assistants.

What this means for you is that regardless of your educational background or work experience, you can create a list of credentials based on your parenting skills and your past professional work that could land you a good job in the child-care field. Once you have gained one to two years' experience, you will be able to begin building a resume that will help you progress toward your ultimate child-care goal, whether it be teacher, administrator, or owner-operator of a child-care center of your own.

PROVIDING DAY-CARE FOR SENIORS

If you think home-based care is only for young children, you might be surprised to find out that day-care for senior citizens is one of the fastest growing opportunities in the helping professions today. Thanks largely to advances in modern medicine, over two million Americans are already eighty-five years or older, and the population is increasing every day. For those of us with nurturing talent, elder care is a field that offers exciting new professional careers promising creativity, personal growth, and satisfaction.

Trends today have reversed themselves from just a few years ago when middle-aged children routinely chose to put their aging parents into residential nursing homes. Many people today opt for keeping their older relatives at home and taking advantage of elder-care centers while they work. Adult day-care facilities are patterned after child-care centers, and many are operated in providers' homes. As long as your house is accessible to wheelchairs and walkers and you are able to provide food service, professional staff, and appropriate activities, you can apply for an operating license and get started. There is such a demand for this timely service that even with minimal word-of-mouth advertising you may find you have more clients than you can handle.

If this idea appeals to you, you will need well-developed administrative abilities along with a strong emotional bond with older people and excellent people skills. Some couples have found that husband/wife teams make good sense in a business like this and pool their talents and interests together. Others have found that partnering with a close friend or compatible business associate gives them the support they need. Still others have made the commitment on their own and operate their facility solo.

Two organizations can be particularly useful in helping you get started. One is the National Institute of Adult Day Care, 409 Third St., S.W., Washington, D.C. 20024; the other is the Older Woman's League, 686 Eleventh St., N.W., Suite 700, Washington, D.C. 20001.

Chapter
Twelve

ON YOUR OWN:
STARTING A SMALL
BUSINESS

Y ou probably never would have gone to your high school reunion if an old classmate hadn't called to ask about your plans and suggest carpooling with two other friends from your senior year study group. No, you hadn't signed up yet, you remember saying, but perhaps you would consider it, now that there would be people to see there.

After that it all just sort of fell into place, your old study partners happy about the idea and the carpool seemingly establishing itself on its own with you as the driver. And the night of the reunion you find yourself not only at the party but enjoying yourself, much to your surprise, standing there in the middle of a group of old friends, laughing like a lunatic at the same old senior-year jokes.

Soon you can't remember the last time you had such a good time. Someone fills your glass and you look around and realize that you know practically everyone in the room. You don't know how it happened after so many years, how all these people who are decades older than when you first met them all still look the same to you as they did then.

You swap stories about spouses, children, travels, jobs. Many of your old friends have children in college now, just like you; some are already grandparents; others are struggling with new families, stepchildren, dependent parents, divorce. Everyone is working, or looking for work, but no one feels secure. Some have been downsized. Others fear they will be by year's end. You are surprised by how many of your classmates are in business for themselves. Professors, engineers, corporate executives, even a dentist who gave up medicine to become a sculptor. Many are successful; most show guarded optimism; some profess wildly profitable years, yet all are enjoying running their own show.

They are all babbling at once now, but you are thoughtful, distracted. You have always wanted to turn your interest in bookbinding into a home-based business. At every book fair you eyed the vendors, wondering how much they produce, how much they sell. You have organizational skills, contacts, drive. You have money saved up and nothing more worthwhile to invest in than yourself. You could scale back your job to half-time or turn it into freelance while you got started.

And with the sweet taste of freedom on your lips you suddenly have a million questions to ask your entrepreneurial classmates.

Living the Dream

If you are intrigued by the thought of being your own boss, developing your own ideas into projects and keeping the lion's share of the money you earn, you are in good company. Every year millions of people get bitten by the entrepreneurial bug and get a mild (or sometimes severe) case of the I-gotta-go-out-on-my-own disease, a somewhat flulike virus that can cause high fever if not treated immediately by either complete bedrest or a small business loan from the local bank and a one-year down payment on an office condo and a color fax machine.

It can be hard for some people to leave the structure and security of a long-term position with a company they know and respect, and which returns the sentiments. But you feel sure you can give up the paycheck, the interactions with colleagues, even the self-defining job title for that world of freedom and the chance to run with your own ideas.

Some days it feels like time is running out, as though if you don't take the chance now you will never have it again. Other days you wonder if the security would be too hard to give up. But then it can feel as if you are all locked up, albeit by the golden handcuffs of salary, prestige, retirement benefits, an expense account—in other words, everything you have ever dreamed of and now do not find to be enough.

You know you should make a plan, and you promise yourself you will sit down with your spouse this Saturday, early in the morning, and talk it through. Can you handle the stress? Can your family finances take the hit? Can you cover your medical insurance until you are making a profit? Do you have the right personality to be on your own? Do you have the potential for success? It's time to find out.

First Things First: Making a Business Plan

Your business plan is a blueprint for your company, a carefully crafted guide to the procedures you will follow to define your concept and turn it into a workable entity. You can't proceed without it, and you shouldn't even try. You need to have everything down on paper before you take even the first tottering steps on the entrepreneurial path.

To begin constructing the plan, first lay out a detailed description of your goal. What will be your main product or service? How will you create or manufacture it? How will you let people know it is available? How will you get it to the marketplace?

Next, think of how you will structure your business. Do you plan to work alone or form a partnership? Will you need to hire personnel, or can you use outside contractors? How will it be organized? Where can you find competent legal and accounting advice?

Make a sharp analysis of your competition. Does your product already exist? Are you planning to improve on similar products already on the market? If so, how is your product better? How can you communicate this to potential buyers? What percent of market share will you aim for? How will you achieve it?

Now project your sales, expenses, and cash flow for the next year as best you can. How much financial backing do you need? Do you have sufficient funds to invest in your business and cover your expenses at the same time? What potential sources of credit do you have?

Detail your equipment needs, including office space and projected transportation needs for the first year. What will you have to buy? Where will the funding come from? What income do you need to break even at the end of the first year? What expenses can you cut if needed? Which are fixed and immutable?

Now think about creative names for your company. Will you name it after your product? Your service? Yourself? Are others already using this name in another field? Can the name be easily remembered?

All this information goes into your business plan. Once you have put it down on paper, you will have a good, clear definition of your goals and your method of achieving them. Make a timetable for what you hope to achieve, and decide when it is feasible to start.

Steering Toward the Future

You will find your business plan indispensable when you speak to the bankers, business associates, friends, relatives, and venture capitalists whom you hope will help fund your enterprise. Finding capital funding is likely to be your first formal step, and to do this you need to know how to convince people to invest in your idea. Having it all down on paper will help.

Your business plan will also be a valuable tool for you as your business progresses. Checking back frequently will help you stay on course; if you have laid out your financial plans in an organized manner you will find it easier to keep accurate records and see if you are on target. If it turns out that your financial forecasts do not dovetail with reality all the time, you will still have an important aid in predicting next year's figures when the time comes to work on projections.

Many worthwhile software programs have been designed to help entrepreneurs set up their financial records, and most are available for under $100. Use them to help periodically review your progress and reassess your direction based on your experiences. Frequent evaluations are necessary to make sure you stay on track with your finances and do not run up debts you will be hard pressed to cover.

Talk to everyone you can find who is in a similar business and learn from their mistakes. Join a professional association in your field if one exists. Look over your colleagues' strong points and compare them to yours; do the same for their weak points. Analyze why your competitors succeed or fail, and look for bad habits in yourself that might interfere with your success. Consider whether you need more education to increase the potential of making your business a success. Realize you do not have to sign up for an MBA degree if all you need to learn are the basics of accounting.

Business research shows that it generally takes between four and six months to make a first sale, nine months to move into the black and a full year to gain a sense of confidence that a business will succeed. Be certain that you have the ability to withstand the uncertainty of that first year by giving yourself sufficient financial and psychological backing to not lose faith while your start-up is taking root.

PROFILE OF A SUCCESSFUL SMALL BUSINESS OWNER

What characteristics do you need to run your own business? Without a doubt, a willingness to work long hours is a primary prerequisite. Despite the fact that corporate work often entails weekends in the office and overnight travel, the biggest change most small business owners report once they have left their job and set up their company is that they now feel they are working twenty-four hours a day.

For many this is not a problem; they love their work and want to do it all the time. But if this is not the way you envisioned your life, you may want to rethink your choice. On the other hand, if you are more interested in the freedom afforded you by working on your own and are willing to make financial trade-offs and seek limited success, you may be able to find the right balance to satisfy all your needs.

In any case, you will need a lot of energy and a high level of initiative to go out on your own. You must be a self-starter—no one is going to get you going in the morning, and if you do not have the self-discipline to sit down at your desk again after a long lunch there will be no work accomplished in your office in the afternoon. You must possess an inner drive and a well-calibrated personal time clock to make yourself succeed on your own.

Another important characteristic is your ability to persevere even in adverse conditions. Small business owners hear the word no day in and day out, just as sales professionals do. A strong ego and well-developed inner sense of purpose are necessary to slough off the accompanying feelings of rejection. If hearing no makes you crumble, then running your own business is not the best work arrangement for you. Find a more supportive environment for your work efforts.

Good leadership skills are essential to running a business, but these can be hard to define. Perhaps the most important skill in this panoply of talents is the ability to motivate others. Hopefully the business you start with yourself as the sole worker will one day grow into an office full of dedicated employees. By then it is too late to find out you can't direct them effectively. This is a skill you should realistically assess in yourself now and develop further if you find you need to.

To keep your inventory in order and maintain an organized marketing effort, you need to possess a range of organizational skills, all of which you can learn if you are motivated. Organizational skills go hand in hand with a high level of industriousness and provide a solid base for executive decisions. You must be able to make good choices using a combination of sound reasoning and highly developed intuition. Your future will depend on it.

Understanding Taxes

Don't feel you have to throw out all your work and return to the corporate world if you find your business is not doing as well as you would like after six months. Take a look at how your tax structure has changed and whether your income strategy can be refreshed.

If you are working from home, have you factored in all the tax breaks you might qualify for? This can mean extra cash for you because some of your personal expenses may now become business deductions. But remember that home-office rules are strict, and to qualify you must keep a part of your house exclusively for business, and you must be able to document that you do so on a regular basis.

Using the dining room table as an office does not qualify! Preferably you have a separate room that you do not use for anything else, a room where you meet clients, customers and vendors, a space that is set up at all times for business.

For a legitimate home office, you are permitted to deduct depreciation plus a prorated portion of the amount it costs you to operate your household. This reduces the taxable income you get from your business. In terms of expenses, you can deduct all the reasonable expenditures of running your business—postage, office supplies, a portion of travel and entertainment costs, legal expenses, insurance costs, printing, telephone charges, even books and magazines that relate to your work and courses that you take to enhance your skills. Furniture and machinery can be depreciated over the course of several years or deducted as a whole expense the first year.

The Benefits of Family Workers

When your child comes home from college on vacations, you can hire him or her to work in your business and shelter some of your income from tax. These wages can be deducted from your income as legitimate business expenses, and each child is allowed to earn a set amount of money each year tax-free. There is a specified dollar amount of a child's income that is automatically sheltered from tax by the standard deduction, and an additional amount of salary can be put into an IRA and also sheltered from tax. These amounts vary every year; check periodically with your accountant to find out the most current figures.

Although family work arrangements are perfectly legal, the IRS is always cautious when they are spotted on tax returns, so it is a good idea to make sure that you are above suspicion at all times. This means keeping good—no, impeccable—records. Nothing is more demoralizing in the first year of a business than a tax audit. Nothing! So carefully document the hours your child works and the exact duties performed for the business, be they filing, computer work, making spreadsheets, writing marketing manuals, taking inventory, or creating new product ideas.

If you have other employees, make sure you do not favor your child over them and treat them all with equal respect. Jealousy of special privileges given to your child—or certain other employees—will create an unhealthy atmosphere that is sure to undo much of the goodwill you work so hard to create.

FINDING CLIENTS AT COLLEGE

When it comes to making a name for yourself, think networking. You want the widest possible range of people to know about your new business venture. Many prime networking situations occur on college campuses, and the school your child attends might be useful for your business start-up. Most colleges and universities sponsor or host conferences on a variety of topics, and many are open to the public. Contact the school and ask to be put on the events calendar mailing list. Read both the local newspaper and the campus publication to find out about upcoming events. Check the school website periodically.

Invest in professional business cards and a flyer announcing the opening of your business and fully describing your product and service, your credentials, and your business goals. Whenever you attend one of these events, bring along a good supply of cards and flyers to hand out to prospective clients.

Offer to serve as a speaker at a conference on a topic related to your business. This will enhance your credibility and set you up as an authority in your area of expertise, and being known will encourage sales for your business.

Don't forget the networking potential of alumni associations at schools from which you have graduated. When you have common bonds with people, they will be more likely to trust you when it comes to doing business. Most likely your alma mater has alumni chapters across the country that hold conferences and social gatherings. These are wonderful networking opportunities. If you were in a fraternity or sorority or other type of social group in college, this membership is likely to inspire a particularly strong kind of loyalty you can tap into to create interest in your business.

Alumni magazines are an off-the-beaten-path place to advertise and establish even more networking contacts. Look up long-lost contacts from your school days and send them your flyer and business card. Make a list of alumni who are mentioned and find out their addresses. Even if you don't know them personally you already have something in common because of your college experience.

When you visit your child in college, find out if there are any continuing education classes in your field. Seminars, workshops, and even graduate programs can supply you with a list of professionals who are updating their skills and might make good business contacts for you because they are already interested in the area you wish to target. Faculty members and department sponsors who administer these programs are also good networking contacts. Check out these contacts at colleges and universities in your home community too.

Liability Limitations

Anytime you hire employees you become responsible to a degree for their health and welfare. They must be safe on the job at all times, and it is up to you to make sure there are no grounds for a charge of injury. Because of this you will want to consider incorporating your business in order to limit your personal liability in case things go wrong.

There are several ways you can do this. You can reduce your liability exposure by setting up either an "S" corporation, through which your profits and losses will be passed on to shareholders, or a "C" corporation, which is the right kind of structure for businesses that make a profit.

Another choice is a limited liability company, which acts like a regular corporation in that it gives you the benefit of reduced liability but is taxed as a partnership. This means all profits and losses are passed through to the tax return of the shareholders or business owners.

Whichever structure you choose will be dependent on more than just your expected profit and loss statement for your first year of operation. How you set up your corporate structure has long-term implications for your projected business gains and expenditures. However, you are not locked into any one structure, and as your needs change so can your organization.

RESOURCES FOR BUSINESS RESEARCH

For step-by-step guidance in the art of becoming an entrepreneur, these three outstanding books will be most useful. Each has its own strengths, and taken together they provide the practical advice, motivation, and solid business education you will need to get started and keep your business going.

The Entrepreneur's Road Map to Business Success, by Lyle Maul and Dianne Mayfield, Saxtons Rivers Publications, 1990. Avoid the dangers, pitfalls, and wasteful detours that deflect your attention from your business goals by gaining a thorough understanding of the risk-taking and financial planning skills you need to develop to insure a flourishing business. Team-written by an entrepreneur and an attorney.

The Four Routes to Entrepreneurial Success, by John Miner, Berrett-

Koehler Publishers, 1996. Learn how personal achievers, sales professionals, managers, and idea experts all differ in their approaches to founding and running a successful business and which patterns and guidelines work best for each type.

Starting Your Business, by Peter Hingston, Dorling-Kindersley, 2001. Follow this authoritative guide to discover how to identify and target your market, uncover unusual sources of financing, sell effectively, keep accurate records, and understand your legal obligations.

PART IV

Family Finance
Reform

Chapter
Thirteen

UPDATE YOUR
INVESTMENT
STRATEGIES

Lining up at the ATM has never been your idea of a great Saturday night. But you were halfway to the movies when you realized you'd spent all your cash at the drugstore and wouldn't be able to pay for tickets, so a swift U-turn brought you to the bank. You just didn't expect a line. Like everyone else, you're drumming your fingers and tapping your foot, waiting for the patrons in front of you to finish so you can take your turn at the cash machine.

You stand there, looking for something—anything!—to do, when you see a sign across the bank lobby advertising a free investment seminar on Wednesday night and a sign-up sheet that has attracted its own little lineup. You're reading the date and time and content of the seminar when the endless line finally moves and you punch in your numbers, get your cash, and walk over there to see what it's all about.

The sign announces that in addition to learning how to invest wisely in stocks, bonds, and mutual funds, the first twenty-five people to sign up will be eligible to win a prize in a free drawing on the night of the seminar. Nothing to buy! Winner gets free financial counseling! You scan the list on the clipboard hanging under the placard and see that two of your PTA friends have entered their names, friends with kids in college like you.

Mentally you check your calendar. You are free next Wednesday night. Why not sign up? You pick up the pen at the end of the little string attached to the clipboard. You begin to scribble your name when you see the topic of the seminar: Investing for the Second Half of Your Life.

You feel your fingers stop writing. Second half of your life? Me? No. I'm just one step past driving my kids to soccer practice, for heaven's sake; the kids are just a few measly years past single-digit birthdays. But my friends on the list—they're not any older than I am. What are they doing there? What am I doing here? I'm not in the second half of my life already.

Am I?

Stocks, Bonds, and Cash Equivalents

A sound investment strategy gives you the means to accomplish what you want in life, especially as you age. Strategic investing isn't just about accumulating wealth; it's about having the chance to work, play, study, travel, and support your dreams and those of your family. By mastering the financial part of your future in your middle years, you widen your choices and give yourself the best chance to accomplish your goals.

People who did not like worrying about money in their early adulthood will not like it any more once they reach their middle years. But errors made in the early years often had the time to be corrected; mistakes made today may not enjoy that luxury. Business research shows that among people between the ages of forty-five and fifty-five, nearly 60 percent believe that their Social Security benefits and pensions will be the major sources of income for them once they retire. The truth is these sources of income will actually cover only about 35 percent. The rest must come from wise investments.

The best way to start making a realistic financial plan is to first determine where you stand; that is, to look at your current asset allocation and see exactly how much money you have put where. Those with sound investment strategies will benefit as much as those who have accumulated money through admittedly slapdash methods, for both will end up with a clear view of reality on which to build an effective strategy.

To accomplish this, begin by making a list of the three classes of investments: stocks, bonds, and cash equivalents. You will include all your investing dollars—your entire portfolio—in these categories. This means everything you have in retirement accounts, as well as regular brokerage accounts, both tax-deferred accounts and regular accounts. Remember to include the balances in your savings and checking accounts too.

Now find out the current market value of each of your investments and put them in the appropriate investment class. Add all the stocks and stock mutual funds together; then add up all the bonds and bond mutual funds, your fixed-income allocation. Now calculate the total of your checking and savings accounts, your money market funds, treasury bills and CDs, your cash equivalents. Calculate the percentage of your portfolio of each of the three classes. These figures will tell you your current asset allocation. Once you know what it is, you are ready to set a strategy.

Measuring Your Fiscal Fitness

Unlike the strength, flexibility, and power of your muscles, your investment portfolio should not be doomed to grow weaker by the mere passage of time. If anything, it should get bigger and better as the years go on. But not everyone knows that the investment strategies that worked so well when you were a young adult are not the same as the ones that produce a strong portfolio once you have reached your middle years. Just like the exercise routine that kept us supple and strong in adolescence but ceased to please in young adulthood, our investments need new strategic guidance to stay healthy as time goes by.

For example, as a working couple in your thirties you probably chose an aggressive strategy for your investments. With many years ahead of you in which to manage your portfolio's growth, you probably balanced your assets with about 30 percent blue chip growth funds or stocks, 30 percent small-company funds or stocks, and perhaps another 30 percent bonds for good interest rates. The 10 percent balance most likely remained in money market accounts or CDs for immediate access.

However, financial experts advise changing the balance of your investments as you age. By the time you reach forty-five or fifty and hopefully have accumulated substantial assets, they recommend adding an element of safety to the mix. A less aggressive portfolio might look like this: 40 percent blue chip growth funds or stocks, 10 percent small-company funds or stocks, 30 percent high-yield bonds, and 20 percent money market accounts. The mix will change again when you approach sixty-five and begin to think about retirement.

The difference between the two types of asset allocations is the balance between safety and risk. Blue chip stocks and funds provide steady and reliable but moderate growth; small company stocks and funds offer growth that is more unpredictable and risky but could be potentially more profitable. Bonds provide a good yield with higher-than-average interest rates and a degree of built-in safety.

Many experts believe that the most important part of a successful investment strategy is not your market timing or your investment choices but the allocation of your assets. It is this overall strategy that is crucial to the health of your long-term investment return.

Different personalities will tend to make different kinds of investments throughout their lives, but all must reconsider their selection process as they age. To keep our portfolios healthy, we must look at the age of our family, our immediate financial goals, and our long-range interests and balance the ratio of growth stocks versus fixed-income investments that we purchase. Financial experts strongly advise that we start this reassessment the month our last child leaves for college or at age fifty, whichever comes first, and rebalance our portfolio every five years.

WHAT THE EXPERTS SAY ABOUT INVESTING

"The long-term trend of the stock market in the United States has always been up. Over time, stocks have outperformed all other kinds of investments, including bonds, CDs and U.S. government securities."

—*Charles Schwab, founder and CEO of*
one of the nation's largest financial services firms

"You, too, can invest wisely. But first you have to forget about the magic bullet, the pot of gold, the secret formula that will make you instantly rich. The real secret is that there is no secret."

—*Lou Altfest, financial planner*

"The best investment is probably the one you live in. The value of a security is the income it is expected to produce over time."

—*Peter Passell, economist*

Selecting Specific Investments

The number of ways to invest your money grows every year, and prospective buyers face a dizzying array of investment opportunities. So how do you decide where to put your money? Finding the answers to several questions about a stock or fund will help you decide if it is a good choice or a potential disaster. The first thing to determine is the investment's annual return and whether it is guaranteed, estimated, or highly variable. You must then match this factor to your expectations and see whether it is acceptable to you.

Next it is necessary to determine the chances for losing the total investment amount and relate that factor to the potential profitability of the investment. This is the basic component of risk and is the most individual decision of all. For some the risk of losing everything will be acceptable based on the potential of gain; for others it will rule out the investment altogether. This is an entirely personal choice and is colored by our own individual view of the world and what we believe we need to do to succeed.

The third factor to consider is the tax consequences of the investment. What are the immediate costs? The future costs? Are they acceptable to you or do you consider them too high to be worth the potential increase in your investment?

Next you should track the performance of this investment over the past several years. Has it kept pace with your other investments? Do you know how it increases in value? Is it liquid enough for your needs? You should fully understand any kind of fees or penalties that will be assessed if you need to get your money out of the investment at a moment's notice. If it locks up your funds for a number of months or years, you must be able to live with this fact to make it worthwhile.

Finally, you should consider whether your portfolio is sufficiently diversified to enable you to withstand the natural ups and downs of the market. Make sure you have included investments of many different types and sources and that the proportions of each match the financial goals that are optimal for your stage of life.

Help With Your Finances

If you find it hard to stay current on financial research and investing news and don't want to be bothered with checking your portfolio regularly, you might want to find a professional to do these tasks for you. Financial planners monitor performance, suggest rebalancing of asset allocation percentages, find stocks and funds to add to your portfolio, and help you decide when to sell. Some or all of these services might simplify your life. But how do you determine what kind of help would best suit your needs?

Think about how much help you really want. Are you looking for guidance in making an investment plan, or do you want someone to manage your investments for you? These are two very different levels of assistance, and it is important to know yourself well enough to understand which would work best for you.

For example, let's say you want to start with a complete financial evaluation, which would include investment strategy, estate planning, tax planning, and a discussion of your insurance requirements. You could consult a professional who will look at where you are financially and how you got there and then help you devise an investment strategy to get you to the level you want to reach. The financial planner will take into account your age and family situation, your job and retirement plans, the level of risk with which you are comfortable and a host of other factors that make up your financial picture. Then he or she will draw up a plan for you that you will put into action and monitor yourself.

Or perhaps you want not only a plan but a financial manager too. There are two types of managers who do this type of work: discretionary and nondiscretionary. The discretionary kind handles the day-to-day investment decisions in your portfolio but allows you to retain control of your assets. He or she has limited power of attorney over

INVESTMENT GLOSSARY: THE ABCS OF FINANCIAL TALK

Understanding the language of investing is the first step toward creating success in your financial future. When you gain a mastery of some of the more common terms in the business section of your newspaper and in stock reports about companies that interest you, you will be able to converse more effectively with financial planners and make more informed investment decisions of your own. Here are a few basic terms to get you started:

Annuity: An investment that promises regular payments over a specific period of time.

Asset: An item of monetary value that is owned by an individual or a company.

Bear market: A market that is in the process of dropping in value.

Blue chip: A large company that is a known market leader, with a solid history of sound finances, increasing earnings, steady dividends, and established brands.

Bond: A debt instrument issued by governments and companies that guarantees it will pay interest to an investor over a specified period of time and return the principal.

Bull market: A market that is rising in value.

Certificate of Deposit (CD): An investment instrument sold by financial institutions that pays a fixed rate of interest for a specific period of time.

COLA: Cost of living adjustment, an annual adjustment on wages and Social Security based on an official rate of inflation, such as the Consumer Price Index.

Common stock: Shares of stock sold to the general public that enable each shareholder to own a percentage of the corporation. Created when a company incorporates.

Compounding: Principal that grows when left to gather interest. Increases as interest accrues on the interest.

Consumer Price Index (CPI): The official inflation rate compiled by the government on a monthly and annual basis. An indicator that reflects changes in prices in the general economy.

your assets and can buy and sell for you without your specific approval for each trade. In a nondiscretionary arrangement, your investment manager gives you advice about strategy and when to buy and sell which stocks, but you do the actual trading yourself.

You might choose a financial manager based on expertise in a particular market area that is of interest to you, such as mutual funds. Investment professionals often develop specialties in particular areas of finance, and if these attract you perhaps this is an approach that would work. Say you have a preference for international investments and want to avoid domestic markets altogether. It would be wise to find a professional who is focused on this area, rather than employ a generalist who might be better qualified to advise you on a more diversified portfolio.

If you are considering an ongoing involvement, think about whether you would prefer working with one specific person or feel more comfortable knowing the resources of the whole firm were available to you but might be administered by people you have never met. Most people have strong preferences when it comes to specific levels of personal contact, and yours are important to take into consideration when selecting a professional to manage your money.

If You Go to a Financial Planner . . .

Setting up a workable investment plan is most effective when you have all the facts and figures that make up your financial life at hand. Before you interview potential portfolio managers, put together all the information you need to complete the picture and bring it with you.

What information do you need? Most important is a full accounting of your assets and liabilities. Simply put, this is everything you own and everything you owe. To this add a list of your monthly expenses, broken down into major categories. You will also need to itemize all sources of income.

If you have thought about retirement and have set goals for yourself, include this information in your accounting. You will need a detailed account of the retirement benefits you will receive from your job. If these vary based on the age at which you retire, include tables for each level. Will you receive any lump sums or will the funds be given to you in installments, or both? Record this information if you have it.

Now explain your family situation—are you married? Divorced?

Widowed? What are the ages of your children? How many are still in school? For those who are still dependent on you, how much do you spend each month in support? How much longer will college tuition payments last? What about graduate school? If you support elderly parents or other relatives, or expect to in the future, make sure to mention this.

Put down the details of your insurance policies—life, health, disability—all the types of insurance that you own. List how much you pay in premiums for each and what the policy is worth. If you know specifically how long you have held each policy, include that information also.

Finally, think about your attitude toward risk and write a paragraph about it. This one issue, of course, has the most impact on how you make your investment decisions. The risk-comfort spectrum goes all the way from people who won't stomach losing even one dollar regardless of how little money they earn to those who are willing to risk nearly all their money for the chance that it will grow tremendously.

Most people, of course, are somewhere in between, preferring to mix safe and steady investments with high-risk, high-potential ones. How you choose to balance safety and growth will determine how you approach your investment strategy. Make sure your financial manager honors your view and will support your decisions wholeheartedly. If he or she does not, find a new manager. You do not want to be guided toward investment decisions you will later regret.

QUIZ: WHAT'S YOUR TOLERANCE FOR RISK?

Ask yourself these ten questions and record your answers, giving yourself five points for every "yes" answer. Then see below to assess your comfort level.

1. You believe you've got to spend money to make money.
2. If the value of your assets changes over the short-term, it doesn't bother you.
3. You are very concerned about finding a hedge against inflation, and you don't mind if it costs a little money to insure that.
4. If you went to Las Vegas on a vacation, you would walk right past the dollar slot machines and head for the $25 blackjack tables.

5. Even when the news is bad and financial experts start predicting a fall in the markets, you are not tempted to purchase safer securities.
6. You are willing to trade a guarantee on your principal if you can get higher long-term growth potential on your investments.
7. You have arranged a trip to Europe and choose to travel standby with a rate that will fall somewhere between $400 and $600 instead of locking in a guaranteed price of $500.
8. You have a good instinct for when to buy and sell securities and tend to do so at the right time.
9. You would be happy to keep all your investments for many years as long as there is high potential for growth.
10. Your apartment building is converting to co-ops, and you have to opportunity to buy your apartment and the one next door. You purchase both.

If you scored in the forty-five- to fifty-point range, you are an aggressive investor who searches out opportunities to make your money grow, even if the odds many not be in your favor. Your attitude toward money is that it exists to make more money, not to be put away to grow safely and slowly. You have a high tolerance for risk and can afford to have a large proportion, perhaps as much as 50 percent, of risky but potentially high-yield securities in your portfolio.

Those who scored between thirty-five and forty points are in the semiaggressive category—willing to take a chance with money only with sufficient information to cushion their risk. If you fall into this category, keep your portfolio well within the asset allocation balances outlined for your age group.

Scores between twenty and thirty points show a conservative investor who does not want to take chances with his or her money, despite the fact that no big rewards can be won. You should always keep a high proportion (40 to 50 percent) of your portfolio in blue chip stocks.

Chapter Fourteen

THE FINE ART OF
SAVING MONEY

Dogs, dogs, beautiful dogs. You can't help thinking about all the pooches, hounds, canines, and just plain hairy beasts you watched with such interest at the kennel club show in town earlier this afternoon. Fancy dogs, rugged dogs, jump-on-your-lap dogs, sly dogs, sturdy dogs, gussied-up-for-the-show dogs. Everywhere you looked, another big drooler, another little yipper, some so adorable they were nothing more than four legs, a pair of eyes and a little pink bow on top of the head.

It's a good thing it was a competition and not a sale, you tell yourself as you walk home through the spring sunshine. The park is gorgeous today with the rhododendrons in bloom, spilling their lush color over fences and bushes and onto the sidewalk. It is easy to imagine one of the fluffy little pooches scampering ahead of you on a leash, trying to pull you down the park path for a romp or over to the bunch of squirrels for a healthy chase. You imagine stroking silky ears and a velvety head, listening to the swish of a tail as it wags in contentment, shaking the whole dog in its effort to show you its pleasure in your touch.

Growing up, you had the usual variety of small pets. You often asked for a dog, but what you got were birds, fish, and hamsters. When your children were small, you promised them a dog but never followed through. It seemed like too much work then, but now, with no more kids at home and a space in your heart the size of Texas, perhaps you should reconsider.

As you enter the park you feel a flutter in your heart, then the familiar pulling back. You're not much of a risk taker, never have been. You don't seek change; you never take chances if you don't have to. You even keep your money in a savings bank, monitoring interest rates and comparing the terms of CDs from one bank to another. And you have done pretty well so far.

But a dog . . . now that wouldn't have to be such a big change. You could carry it around in a little backpack if it rained or snowed and it didn't want to get its feet wet. It wouldn't have to be that much work, now would it?

Playing it safe has always worked so well for you though. Hasn't your money grown steadily all these years, all because you know how to keep your savings safe? But as you leave the park you find yourself thinking that maybe it's time to make a withdrawal, a small one of course. A warm, wiggly puppy—now that's worth having saved for all these years.

Getting the Most for Your Banking Dollar

Every investor's portfolio, no matter how aggressive or conservative the owner, needs to contain a provision for liquid assets. These are cash equivalents that can be turned into money in your pocket in a matter of hours to help you deal with emergencies, must-have purchases, and other unforeseen events that require immediate funds.

Financial professionals advise that you keep a minimum of 10 percent of your investment portfolio in the bank, and they recommend that families put away at least six months' income in liquid assets. But how can you make saving money worthwhile when interest rates are low and you need a decent return on your money?

The key is to look closely at each savings vehicle and see how best to combine them to suit your needs most effectively. There are three fundamental factors you should consider in your evaluation: risk, which defines the safety of your investment; liquidity, or how readily available your money is; and yield, the amount your savings grow through interest. All these factors are interdependent, and there is no one vehicle that offers the benefits of all three.

Let's look at risk first. The market rewards investors for taking two basic types of risks—default and market risk. You can avoid default by keeping your savings in an account insured by the federal government or by buying government-insured securities, such as savings bonds. Market risk comes into play in savings that pay a fixed interest rate, such as fixed-rate CDs, and becomes more or less of a factor based on the date of maturity. Market risk increases as the date of maturity of the financial instrument moves further into the future, as this enables the interest rate to rise, thus making the market value of your investment decline.

You can avoid market risk by purchasing variable-rate savings options—CDs and money market funds, for example, which are risk-free because their rate changes with the market.

The next factor is liquidity. For ease of liquidity, you can't do better than a checking account, which is payable on demand. Most people believe savings accounts are equally liquid, but the fact is banks can make depositors wait for savings account withdrawals if they so choose. Securities traded on the open market, such as treasury bills, are somewhat less accessible than savings accounts because the transactions can take time. CDs issued by savings banks, credit unions, and commercial banks have about the same degree of liquidity, since most issuers will redeem them for cash before they mature.

Yield is the third major factor affecting your choice of savings options. The rate of return on your investment is determined by the method used to compute the interest and frequency with which the interest is compounded. Most of the time, high liquidity means low yield. High risk means higher yield. But assets with higher risk also have less liquidity.

How Fees Factor In

The bottom line in choosing the best combination of savings options is finding the correct balance among the risk, yield, and levels of liquidity available to you. But as the range of choices widens, additional factors come into play that make the decision more complex.

Any financial instrument that you buy or sell has fees associated with it, and these can dramatically affect the price of the transaction. Flat fees accompany all treasury security transactions under $100,000, and some banks and brokerage houses charge as much as $100 to buy or sell a treasury bill. Can you beat these fees? Yes. Shop around for discount brokers, or buy securities directly from the Federal Reserve.

Even savings accounts have associated fees, charged by both commercial banks and savings and loan associations. Inactive accounts and accounts closed shortly after they are opened can incur charges, and some banks charge customers if there has been no activity for ninety days. Others attach a fee for ATM withdrawals and deposits or for money withdrawn from an account more than twice a month.

Negotiability and expandability are two qualities of savings instruments that can look attractive, but you must make certain you understand them fully to use them to your advantage. Negotiable accounts are those you can sell to a third party. Nonnegotiable instruments cannot be sold on the open market, but they can be exchanged for cash at the institution that issued them. Money market funds are negotiable, as are treasury securities, but savings accounts and CDs under $100,000 are not.

When you purchase a bond or CD, you have bought a savings vehicle that is nonexpandable. This means you cannot add to the principal, and in some cases you are not even permitted to reinvest the interest you have earned. Money market accounts, however, can be added to at any time, although some restrict the amount you can add at one time. In most money market accounts, interest can be reinvested.

Negotiate for Better Service

How important is convenience to you, and are you willing to pay for it if necessary? For example, do you want your bank to withdraw a set amount from your checking account each month and deposit it into your money market or savings account? Some banks will do this for you; others will not. Most banks do not charge a fee for these automatic transfers, but some do.

All banks have established minimum investment amounts, and they vary with the institution and savings vehicle. You will have different options if you want to place an initial deposit of $5000 or $50. But if the bank that is most convenient to you says no, try negotiating. Some banks offer special services such as free checking accounts or free checks for a fee account. If you want a service that is not offered at your investment level, suggest foregoing another service for which you qualify in exchange.

The Six Major Savings Options

Becoming thoroughly familiar with the products offered by your bank will help you save money. The most common savings instrument is the regular savings account, offered by commercial banks, credit unions, and savings banks. All you need is a small initial deposit, sometimes as low as $10, and you can make deposits or withdrawals anytime you wish. But be careful of fees imposed by the bank, especially charges for maintaining a low balance, which sometimes can even exceed the interest the account earns. As a rule, savings accounts pay low interest rates, but the money in your account is almost as liquid as cash itself and at almost all banks depositors are insured by the federal government.

Money market accounts are generally a better alternative but require larger initial deposits and higher minimum balances to avoid fees. Interest rates are higher than on savings accounts, and depositors are often allowed to write checks from their accounts.

While money market accounts are issued by banks, money market funds are offered by companies regulated by the Securities and Exchange Commission. The yield of these funds changes daily, as they are invested in treasury bills, negotiable CDs issued by commercial banks, and other short-term financial instruments. These funds usually pay higher yields than money market accounts but require a higher initial deposit, usually $1000. Their major drawback is that they are not insured by the federal government, but the risk of default is very small since the funds are invested in very conservative instruments.

Savers interested in certificates of deposit can usually invest as little as $500 and enjoy a yield that is almost always higher than what you would get in money market funds, money market accounts, or regular savings accounts. The yield rises with the amount invested, so a larger investment will naturally have a greater interest rate. CDs are offered by commercial banks, credit unions, and savings banks and are insured by the federal government. However, your money must remain on deposit for a specified time period or a penalty must be paid, thus lowering the liquidity of your investment. The longer you can leave your money in the CD, the better the yield.

Like CDs, Series EE savings bonds produce a higher yield the longer the bonds are held and have the advantage of being available at denominations as small as $75, which makes them particularly useful as gifts to commemorate special occasions. The major advantage of savings bonds, however, is that taxes on their earnings do not have to be paid until the bonds are cashed. They offer better yields than CDs or money market instruments, but investors who want to withdraw the funds before the bond matures will unfortunately suffer a severe penalty. Savings bonds are a favorite gift to young people who have little need for liquidity and stand to benefit fully from the relatively high interest rates.

Investors interested in short-term treasury securities can purchase them through a bank or broker or directly through the Federal Reserve Bank, which has offices in most major cities. Treasury securities come in three types: notes, bonds, and bills, each issued with different maturities and in different denominations. Safe and liquid, these securities are exempt from all state and local taxes except estate taxes. They do carry a fair amount of market risk, however, as all debt securities do, as they are sold on the open market at competitively determined interest rates.

HOW SAFE IS YOUR BANK?

Banks make their money by taking the difference between the interest they pay depositors and the much higher interest they charge borrowers and keeping it. Because banks want to have long-term deposits they can count on, they are willing to pay higher rates for long-term CDs, which have penalties if you withdraw them early. On the other hand, savings account deposits, which can be withdrawn at a moment's notice, pay less interest.

Banks are willing to give a higher yield to large balances kept on account because the cost of maintaining a customer's account is the same whether it is large or small, and they make more money on the larger one. In addition, they pay less interest on money market mutual funds, which have no federal insurance and are less secure.

All national banks are required by law to be members of the Federal Deposit Insurance Corporation, the federal organization that protects depositors up to certain maximum amounts. State chartered banks are not required to join, but most do. According to the FDIC charter, a $100,000 maximum applies to all deposits in any one bank if they are under the name of the same individual. Depositing under your Social Security number instead of your name will yield the same protections.

For example, if you have deposits of $75,000 in CDs, $30,000 in money market accounts and $12,000 in checking at the same bank, only $100,000 of the $112,000 would be protected. But there is a way to extend your coverage: you can open another account at a different bank that is not a branch of the first, or a second set of accounts as a joint owner with a child or a spouse. If each group of accounts is registered under a different owner, they will each be protected up to $100,000.

However, the FDIC does not guarantee that you will be able to withdraw your money when you demand it. The bank has the right to require depositors to give advance notice of their intention to withdraw funds. Under the terms and conditions governing savings accounts, up to thirty days advance notice can be required to protect the bank in critical cash flow situations.

While some investors believe that big banks are safer than small ones because they are better protected from the chance of failure, everyone who is concerned about the safety of their money can examine a few financial ratios and determine the fiscal health of their savings institution. The three signs to look for are the amount of capital a bank has, whether the bank has a high proportion of problem loans and whether or not it is making a profit. This information is available to depositors by visiting the bank's administrative offices and asking for the appropriate statistics.

Tips for Savers: More Gain, Less Pain

Economists who study savings patterns among American workers say that almost two-thirds of them have no savings at all, other than the equity in their homes and their pension plans. However, as people age they tend to save more, and the years between ages forty-five and sixty are considered high-savings years. People in this age group become aware of approaching retirement and its attendant reduction in their earning power. They also want more liquidity to help deal with unexpected events, such as the need to loan money to adult children setting up a business or professional practice.

Discipline and creative thinking are necessary to find ways to hold on to the extra dollars slated for savings accounts. Financial planners recommend that people in their thirties save 10 percent of their pretax income, while those who wait until their fifties to begin a regular savings plan will have to put away 20 percent of their pretax income to reach the same savings level, due to the way compounding works.

Of course, none of us can turn back time, but as we enter our middle years we still have the opportunity to take advantage of the miracle of compounding by beginning a steady savings plan. The mathematical phenomenon of compounding will work for us at any age, multiplying our savings to new heights. For example, $1000 put into a long-term investment today at 8 percent interest will yield $1,470 in five years, but in ten years your money will have more than doubled to $2,160.

Understanding Compounding

Compounding raises the effective annual yield on an investment. Why? Simply put, it is the paying of interest on interest. The more frequent the compounding the higher the yield. When you are considering purchasing any savings instrument, first check with the bank to see how often they compound. Most compound daily, but not all do. Some compound quarterly, and others do not compound at all, actually rendering some investments not worthwhile.

Take a $10,000 one-year CD paying 10 percent, for example. With no compounding (also called simple compounding) the interest earned is a flat $1000. Semiannual compounding would yield $1025; quarterly $1038.13, monthly $1047.13, and daily $1051.56. Continuous, which is a form of compounding similar to daily but figured on a slightly different scale, would yield $1051.71. Be sure to check with your bank before you buy to make sure you are getting the maximum compounding benefit.

See It and Save It

To encourage savings, some people need to create gimmicks that help get the nickels and dimes out of their trouser pockets and into the bank. If you are one of these, arrange with your employer to have a specified amount of money taken out of your paycheck each week and automatically deposited in a savings account. As you see the account grow, you will feel a sense of accomplishment that will hopefully spur you on to saving more.

Putting away money this way, before you get to hold it in your hand, is a very effective method of building a nest egg, particularly if the money is deposited in an account with hefty penalties for early withdrawal. This type of account is likely to offer a higher yield than a more liquid account and thus create more growth more quickly.

It is also useful to instruct brokers and fund managers to reinvest dividends and capital distributions as they occur. Because this is money you don't handle, it will not feel like a loss to put it away.

Cutting down on your weekly allowance of spending money can also help savings grow. Even a small amount like $10 a week can add up to significant savings. Lowering credit card debt by either throwing out some of your cards or paying the balance in full each month will also help. Avoiding the 18.5 percent interest charge on your credit card balance will actually produce an annual return of a whopping 28 percent on your money.

If you think of saving as a habit, you will be more likely to begin to do it automatically. Check your savings account periodically to make sure you are putting something away on a regular basis.

FINANCIAL PUBLICATIONS WORTH READING

Just like the regular dental checkups and exercise programs we set up to improve our health, most of us need to establish a system to keep our personal finance knowledge up to date. Reading several well-respected financial journals every month is the best way to learn about changes in the financial world and find out about new research that could affect our investment decisions. Here are five outstanding business publications to help you stay informed:

Fortune Magazine—Published every other week, *Fortune* provides information on taxes, the stock market, and new investment products and offers profiles on major players in the financial world. Best known for its personal investing column.

BusinessWeek—Short, crisp articles cover the business world and provide market summaries and investment outlooks in several areas each week. News about the best places to invest your money is a staple feature.

Barron's—A weekly tabloid, filled with stories about Wall Street and the people who are making names for themselves in the market. Aspects of business or finance are featured each week in primer format, and stock, bond, and options tables appear in every issue.

Money Magazine—A monthly about personal finance that covers the basics of economic issues and individual investing. Carefully researched and very readable, it helps novices understand money supply figures, stock index futures, and stock tables.

The Wall Street Journal—Long considered both the bible of the investment world and America's premier business publication, this national newspaper is issued daily and provides up-to-date reporting on the world of economics and business. Essential reading for any informed investor.

*Chapter
Fifteen*

CAMPUS FINANCES AND
HOW TO MANAGE THEM

I t wasn't easy to drive right past the car dealer with the new Corvettes in the showroom, and to your credit you did manage to make it down the street without stopping. But the attraction you have to beauty, speed, and craftsmanship that has always made you love fine cars got you to turn around, double back, and park your dull but sturdy old Volvo within a stone's throw of the sleek red machines.

You sit in the car now and wonder if you should get out. You feel the strength of your desire to run your hands over the Corvettes' hoods, climb into the leather buckets, hold the wheel. You have time to look, you tell yourself, you just don't have money to buy. But looking is free, you reason. Finally you tuck your wallet and checkbook under the mat for your own protection and take your barely contained excitement into the showroom.

You head right for the convertible, a deep red super-charged machine clothed in a warm claret skin. The leather seats look soft, supple, cushiony. You can hardly resist the urge to climb inside, a pull almost gravitylike in its strength and insistence.

The salesman's approach doesn't trouble you at all now; you are already in the driver's seat when he appears by your side, clipboard in hand. He sees right away he doesn't have to sell you on the merits of the car, but he tells you anyway about the turbo engine and the superior braking system. You try to look as if you're listening as you run damp palms along the shiny burled dashboard, let your feet find the pedals, allow your eyes to wander approvingly over the upholstered gear box.

It is the inevitable spiel about financing that finally breaks through your reverie. You know you can't afford the car. You knew it when you walked in. You have four years of tuition bills to pay, thousands of dollars in college expenses to manage. But you hear him talking about loans, leases, interest rates, repayment plans, once-in-a-lifetime deals. You try not to pay attention, but you find yourself adding up figures in your head.

Soon you are out of the driver's seat and into the visitor's chair, poised over the desk calculator, hopelessly attempting to manipulate the columns of numbers swimming before your eyes. Maybe if you just add up the figures one more time they will come out right. Maybe there's a way to lower those college costs. There's got to be. You simply have to have that car.

Free Money for College

Aside from buying a house, paying for college is the single largest expenditure a family is likely to face during the years they are raising their children. Financial advisors routinely recommend that parents begin to save for college while their children are still in the neonatal ward, and though a few may actually listen to this advice, most are faced with finding a way to pay the staggering costs once their children begin their university education.

Even for those who invested wisely, a volatile stock market can chop off a big chunk of the college nest egg, and a quick look at the business pages of your local newspaper will tell you that college tuition is rising faster than inflation. In-state fees for public colleges and costs for private institutions continue to increase between 5 and 7 percent a year.

To meet these rising expenses, families employ a variety of tactics, shaped by a combination of their financial resources and goals and their personalities. Parents cash in stock investments, liquidate retirement accounts, apply for loans, pursue scholarship grants, or mix and match among these strategies.

The greatest force keeping families from winning more financial aid from both government sources and individual colleges is their mistaken belief that all aid is determined upon the student's acceptance to college and a family's financial situation is never reevaluated. The truth is otherwise; a family's need for financial aid can be reconsidered each year. If you don't qualify for a grant in freshman year, ask again. Students may submit new financial aid requests every spring.

Perhaps your medical expenses have increased dramatically or you have another child in college or graduate school. Maybe your family income has fallen due to a layoff or a business failure. Perhaps you have new expenses or obligations due to caring for an elderly parent. All this should be detailed in a letter to the financial aid office when the application for grant money is submitted.

Make sure you know your school's deadlines and the correct forms to fill out, including the right person to send them to. Circumstances change both in your life and in the life of the college. The school's endowment may increase, leading to more available grant aid, which does not have to be repaid. Income thresholds may be lowered so that you may qualify this year even if you didn't before. And policies that omitted your specific type of request one year may no longer be in place the next.

Another important myth to explode is the one that says that grant offers are written in stone. Not so! If you don't feel you have been given enough, speak up. Write a letter with more details about your financial need. If your business is about to go under, say so directly. Persistence is important, and a polite but assertive approach is warranted. Be courteous but firm in describing your financial situation, and follow up the letter with a phone call.

Outside organizations also provide scholarship support in the form of grants to students who have already begun college. Check with local credit unions in your area, fraternal organizations, military organizations, and community groups to find out whether they fund scholarships based on need, academic merit, community service, or a combination of these, and request application materials and a schedule of due dates.

If you child qualifies for one of these scholarships, and the college wants reduce the grant it offers you as a result, do not allow them to do so. Fight for your right to retain the original amount of grant aid.

You should not be penalized for winning scholarship money from an outside source.

Looking at Loans

Even if you didn't take out a loan to pay for freshman-year tuition, you can decide you want to apply for one for sophomore year. Family circumstances change, and college financial aid officers are sensitive to this. Many colleges offer their own low-interest loans for both incoming and continuing students. Schools particularly want to help students who are already enrolled; it is far less expensive to help fund good students whose financial needs have changed than to lose them and bring in new ones. Students or their parents should approach the financial aid office and ask for information on a specific type of aid called a retention loan.

These loans are especially prevalent on the campuses of medium-priced private colleges. That's because these schools do not have as many applicants as the Ivies or the popular state schools and have to work a little harder to attract and keep their students. There is generally no fee to apply, but most loans do have a yearly limit.

Many families who want to supplement direct loans from their colleges borrow money for tuition from a federal program called the Parent Loan for Undergraduate Students, or PLUS. This loan program is very popular because it enables parents to borrow the entire cost of a college education with no collateral and no demonstrated level of need.

Other types of federal assistance are also available. The low-interest Stafford Loans offer the most widely used plan. The school's financial aid office determines a family's eligibility through the Free Application for Federal Student Aid, the FAFSA. When sufficient need is demonstrated, families are able to obtain the subsidized version of these loans, in which the government pays the interest as long as the student is in school. In the unsubsidized version, students are accountable for all the interest, although payment can be deferred until after graduation.

Repayment on Stafford Loans begins six months after students graduate from college, leave school, or drop below half-time status, and must be completed within ten years. PLUS loans have the same ten-year repayment requirement, but repayment actually begins within sixty days of disbursement. In other words, the parents of a freshman with a PLUS loan would probably have to begin paying back the loan in February or March of their child's first year in college.

Both loan systems offer built-in flexibility for an additional fee, which allows for income-sensitive repayment schedules tied to your earnings at a given point in time, and extended repayment plans, which spread out the loan term beyond the standard ten-year requirement. Students who go on to graduate school are often eligible for deferments that delay the start date for repayment. Within some income limitations, it is possible that the monthly interest you pay on your education loans could be deductible on your federal income tax.

Finding More Dollars for Scholars

In addition to grants and loans, another strategy for containing college costs is to search out ways to stretch the money you do have to spend. One simple tactic that is often overlooked is to call your school's student accounts office and ask if you can pay the tuition by credit card. An increasing number of schools are accepting this new payment option because it increases flexibility for parents and insures timely payment for the school. But there is a bonus for you. In addition to the convenience, a major monetary advantage for you is that it can make you eligible for travel miles and other free benefits.

Think about it. The large chunk of money spent on a few semesters' tuition could probably give you enough free miles to fly halfway around the world. Or if your child attends a college or university far away, it could help purchase several tickets home for vacations. If your school does not currently offer such benefits, you might organize a group of parents to lobby for it. Check with the college development office and see if they will supply you with a list of names. If you can't get any support, make a pitch on your own. It could be your college does not have a credit card policy simply because no one has ever asked for one.

Maintaining your child's entertainment budget on the low end is another good way to control college costs. Encourage your child to attend the many free cultural events on campus instead of taking part in more costly off-campus entertainment on a routine basis. Lectures, visiting arts groups, and student-run productions abound on college campuses and can provide unique and satisfying experiences for your student.

Keep clothing costs down by encouraging your child to wear comfortable, casual clothes during the day and providing him or her with a few unique, up-to-the-minute outfits for special occasions. Most college fashion cultures don't require expensive or dressy clothes, and the chic college wardrobe still consists mainly of jeans, T-shirts, and boots or sandals.

Does your child want to take a trip during spring break? Going away with friends on the annual student migration to warm climes is a part of the college experience most kids don't want to miss. Suggest a car trip instead of an airplane ride to keep costs down, and help your child find a resort that offers student rates. A fancy name may sound good at first blush, but what your child really wants is other college students in residence. Do some research and make recommendations that suit your budget.

Another way to make your money go further is to look for travel bargains for transporting your child between college and home. Airlines and train agencies offer reduced rates for students who travel during certain times and who are willing to buy tickets in bulk. Some have programs for frequent travelers that offer free passage after a specified number of trips.

Set-up costs at the beginning of each academic year can run high, and one way to help keep them down is to take advantage of savings offered by the school. If your child needs a new computer and the college or university is offering a deal on one particular model, it's usually worth buying it. Whenever possible, do your shopping for bed linens, lamps, and shelving at home. Avoiding last-minute purchases at the university store will save you 20 to 25 percent on these common items. Stock up on discount drugstore items at home too, instead of buying them on campus piece by piece at significantly higher costs.

If your school offers a refrigerator rental for the dorm room, this is usually a good bargain, particularly if the cost is split among two or three roommates. Refrigerators enable students to economize on grocery bills and keep fresh food on hand while also helping them to cut down on the amount of junk food bought at the snack bar to assuage late-night hunger. Less junk food means a slimmer waistline and a fatter bank account, two things your child will be grateful for when the semester ends.

Student Credit Cards: Handle With Care

Most students who are just beginning to handle their own money need clear rules and firm guidance about when to spend it, where to spend it, and how to pay the bills. This is especially true when it comes to credit cards. Few students understand the results of unpaid credit card bills and how they can damage their financial well-being.

The American Council of Education says that nearly 80 percent of undergraduates have at least one credit card, and nearly half of them carry an average balance of $1500 from month to month. This results in interest charges of between $250 and $350 a year. Some college administrators have admitted that in extreme cases students have been forced to drop out of college because of credit card debt.

Most colleges and universities allow credit card companies to host tables at orientation and registration offering cards to students, and many permit credit card applications to be put into bags along with items purchased at the bookstore. Most of these credit card companies waive the usual income and employment requirements for college students, making it very easy to qualify for a card. To help your child understand how the card works, let him or her compare several cards' interest rates, annual fees, and the grace period before interest is charged on purchases.

Owning a card and knowing how to use it responsibly are of course very different things. Credit cards do provide advantages to students who might otherwise not be able to make bookstore purchases, arrange for a flight home, or take advantage of special sales, but before granting your child this adult privilege make sure he or she understands your rules and is willing to abide by them.

You might want to allow credit card use for emergencies only, for example, or instruct your child not to use the card for group dinners, as people won't always pay back what they owe. Be certain your child knows the limit of purchases you have set and the overall credit limit on the card. Require him or her to pay a portion of the interest if a bill is not paid on time. Explain that bills paid by the due date will help build a good credit record, but that late bills will do just the opposite.

WORKSHOP: CREATE A CAMPUS SPENDING GUIDE

Making a comprehensive budget for your child's daily college expenses will help provide much-needed guidance for your child's away-from-home financial life. The best way to do this is to sit down together and answer these questions, then reassess your budget over Christmas vacation and once again over spring break and make the appropriate adjustments.

1. How much money will your child have available to spend?
2. Will the money come from your accounts or your child's savings, investments, summer earnings, or campus job, or a set proportion of each?
3. Will the money be available in a checking account or savings account, through a credit or debit card, in cash, or in a specifically determined combination of these?
4. Will you supply your child with money through weekly or monthly deposits, or will you make it available all at once?
5. How much cash should your child keep on hand?
6. Will your child have an ATM card to access the money?
7. What will the money be there to pay for—school supplies, books, transportation, gifts, social activities, snacks, CDs, telephone calls?
8. How much money will be allocated to each budget category?
9. Will your child be accountable to you for all expenditures, or will he or she have the responsibility to manage the money?

The Truth About Student Employment

Getting a job on campus is a great way to learn about money, and many students can easily fit a ten- or twelve-hour weekly shift into their academic schedule. Often students say they come to feel at home on campus more quickly if they work a part of every day, because the job adds an extra measure of involvement to their academic and social life.

Many university departments, programs, and organizations offer jobs to students during the academic year. Kids work in dining services, in the library, the bookstore, athletic departments, computer centers, research labs, public safety offices, health services, grounds and building maintenance, even the admissions office, where they are best known for offering campus tours. Working in the academic department in which a student plans to major is a very good way to get to know the professors in the field and see how they might get involved in their research.

Most campuses post job listings on the school website and the bulletin board at the student employment office, where administrators will help students find work suited to their interests, abilities, and time schedules.

A student who earns his or her own pocket money will spend it with a different degree of thought than if it is merely provided by a generous parent. Because independence is the goal of college students, those who are able to become fully self-supporting tend to relate a higher degree of satisfaction with college life and an easier adjustment to the work world after graduation.

What Students Need to Know About Money

Because of the emotional complexities of parenting teens, teaching them to be financially responsible is often not a priority in many households. But financial planners say that students who go to college already knowing the basics are far less likely to run into common but expensive beginner problems like bouncing checks. Part of your own financial plan to reduce costs at college should include some serious education on financial matters for your child.

There are several ways to do this. For example, consider loaning your child money—say, $100 or so—and charge interest. Draw up a contract and arrange for your child to make monthly payments. Compare how much the loan would cost if it were paid back in one year, two years, or five years. Discuss the value of each option and the reasons why each could be chosen.

The next time you pay bills when your child is home for a weekend or a vacation, let him or her look over your shoulder and explain how much water, gas, electricity, and telephone services cost each month.

Demonstrate how much you would save if you eliminated monthly cable TV charges or canceled magazine subscriptions. Explain why each of these has value to you and why you feel they are worth the extra expense. Show how the figures in your checkbook not only show your purchasing power but stand for the values you and your family hold.

It is important that you teach your child how to balance a checkbook, because no one else will. Have him or her practice recording transactions and figuring the balance, entering and subtracting each check and entering and adding each deposit. Demonstrate how to reconcile the bank statement at the end of each month. Point out that just because you have checks in your checkbook doesn't mean you have money in your account!

At tax time, when you have completed your returns, show your child how you filled out the forms and why you are in a particular tax bracket. Explain how withholding works. Show him or her what portion of your income goes to state, federal, and municipal taxes. Explain how schools and public libraries in your communities are supported by your tax dollars and how much your family contributes. Make sure your child understands how taxes are levied, and how the relationship between political representation and tax assessments works.

COLLEGE FINANCIAL AID RESOURCES

The details of how grant and loan programs operate change from year to year, and it is necessary to work with up-to-date information to create the most effective applications. The following publications will help you gain timely information and teach you what you need to know to formulate the best strategies:

The Student Guide: Five Federal Financial Aid Programs, a reference manual for federal financial assistance updated and issued annually by the Department of Education to explain the rules and deadlines for tuition grants and loans. Available free of charge from the Federal Student Aid Information Center, P.O. Box 84, Washington, D.C., 20044, 800-433-3243.

Peterson's College Money Handbook, published by Peterson's Guides, 2002. A well-known guidebook to take you through the maze of financial planning options and help you find the way best suited to your resources and needs.

Paying for College: A Guide for Parents, by Gerald Krefetz, published by the College Board, 1995. An indispensable tool for understanding the intricacies of the numerous types of financial aid offerings.

Lovejoy's Guide to Financial Aid, by Robert and Anna Leider, published by Simon & Schuster, 2001. Lists and describes hundreds of scholarship opportunities and how and when to apply for them.

Chapter
Sixteen

SECURING YOUR FAMILY'S FINANCIAL FUTURE

The attic still smells like oranges and lemon oil, you notice with a frisson of pleasure as you climb the stairs and enter the warm, dry space beneath the top gable of the house. A light layer of dust sits on everything, turning brown boxes, black trunks, and red cartons the same filmy white color. You can't remember the last time you were up here, and you run your fingers over the stack of wicker baskets in the far corner now and wonder if this is where you'll find the papers you want. You pull out packets of envelopes held together with rubber bands, releasing stock transactions, bank checks, tax documents, but not the documentation you need to prove your child had the requisite immunizations before leaving for college. But you will keep looking. It has to be here somewhere.

You move on to the file cabinet, the big old black one with the two broken handles, and pry open the top drawer, thumbing through the contents of the front folders. Old insurance policies tumble out. Appliance manuals for machines long since assigned to the scrap heap. Tax receipts and mortgage applications from your first house. A savings passbook from a fifteen-year-old account in another state.

You shut the file drawer and blow the dust off a battered old metal case, pulling back the lock mechanism and lifting the lid. There, in a series of well-marked shoeboxes, are stacks of old family photos from when you were young. You can't help sifting through them, and as you do you are stunned to feel the experiences come to life once again: blowing out the candles at your tenth birthday, dancing at your sister's sweet sixteen, staying up all night at the camp reunion pajama party. Your mom with dark hair and your dad with any hair at all are long-forgotten memories, yet here they are in black and white, a little tattered around the edges, but no worse for wear.

Before you know it the little bit of light able to filter through the attic window has vanished, and you are still sitting on the floor in the small circle of electric illumination. You feel surrounded by pictures. It is as if the power of yesterday so fills the space it leaves no room for today or tomorrow. Here you are at the beautiful wedding they somehow managed to give you; there is the first house they helped you buy; here they are at the business they underwrote, the business that has made today's college tuition payments possible.

Slowly you pack up the photos into their boxes, and as you do so you start to gather the papers you have found, the old insurance policies and tax records and stock certificates, the whole paper trail that will someday define what you are able to give your children to help launch them into adulthood the way your parents did for you. There is so much you want to provide for them, but today for the first time you realize the level of care and foresight and ingenuity that your parents employed to make sure it was all there for you when the time came.

You stack all the papers in a box and take them downstairs, along with the folder you hope will contain the immunizations records. Tonight you will sort them out and make sense of them. Tomorrow you will make a plan. You don't know where you will start, but it doesn't matter. Wherever you start it will be the first step.

Ready, Aim, Organize!

Good record-keeping begins the moment you realize that organized legal and financial data naturally falls into a pattern of filing that you can easily control. There are four basic locations for your important papers: a safe-deposit box at the bank, an active storage file at home that is easily accessible, a box or file cabinet stored somewhere in the house, and your attorney's office.

Start by sitting down with your spouse and discussing who will be responsible for maintaining the family files. Will you do it together, or is one of you more able or more willing to do the work? Next, decide who besides the two of you will know the location of all the records. Will it be your children? All of them? Only the oldest? Only the one who lives the nearest? Your attorney? A trusted friend, neighbor, or sibling?

Now choose the bank in which you will open a safe-deposit box. Comparison shop for fees and services before you decide, and discuss how important convenience and location are to you. Most banks offer different size boxes for different fees. Once you select one, you will have to decide where to put the key. Will you keep it on a key ring? Will it go into a desk drawer or do you prefer it hidden in, say, the refrigerator? Will you keep a note to yourself in your bill box with the exact location in case you forget?

Next, decide where to file your active records. If you have a study or a den, this is a logical place. But some people prefer a locked desk in their bedroom, a drawer in the dining room credenza, or even a box under their bed. Anyplace is fine, as long as it is easily accessible. Your inactive files can be stored in a less prime spot, like the basement or garage, as long as it is not so damp there it will encourage mildew to grow on your papers.

Finally, if you have never used an attorney before, now is a good time to choose one. Ask friends and family members in your community for references and arrange consultations to talk about fees and services. Make sure you feel comfortable sharing your most personal legal and financial dealings with him or her. A good attorney quickly becomes a trusted advisor, but one with whom you do not feel a healthy rapport will not be able to serve you as fully as you might ultimately want.

Safe-Deposit Savvy: What's Hot, What's Not

Make sure your attorney's office has copies of all your vital documents. These include the original of your last will and testament, along with your living will, if you have one, and your signed power of attorney statement. If you have filled out an advance medical directive, also known as a durable medical power of attorney or health care proxy, make sure your attorney has this on file.

Many people give their attorneys a copy of their safe-deposit key too. Legal planners recommend that you authorize someone other than yourself to be allowed to open the box to ensure swift access in case an emergency disables you. Your attorney is often the best choice because he or she is working for you and will be available to intervene in your best interests if necessary, but a trusted friend or relative is also fine. If you have contracted for burial plots or prepaid any funeral plans, you should write a letter of instruction detailing your wishes and file this with your attorney also.

Personal papers belong in your safe-deposit box. These papers include birth, death, and marriage certificates and any divorce decrees, plus citizenship papers and your passports. If any members of your family served in the armed forces, their military records and Veterans Administration papers should be stored here too, along with any Social Security documents.

Don't put your will or life insurance policies in the box, because most states require that the bank seal the box if the owner or joint owner dies, thus delaying the settling of your estate. Do add copies of the power of attorney statement and letters of instruction that are filed with your attorney, however.

Check with your bank about whether or not the contents of your box are insured against theft or damage. Most banks do not offer this type of insurance, but some do. Ask your insurance agent if your safe-deposit box contents are covered under your homeowner's policy. If you plan to put jewelry in the box, find out the cost of a floater for valuables you store there.

Pertinent financial papers should also be secured in your safe-deposit box. These include retirement and pension plans, home records such as surveys and site plans, real estate deeds, and the titles to your cars. In addition, keep stock certificates, bonds, and mutual fund documents there.

CHECKLIST: NAMING THE PROFESSIONALS IN YOUR LIFE

It is natural that as we age and accumulate property, our legal and financial lives become more complex. To help keep ourselves organized, it is a good idea to create a list of the people we have hired to help us. It won't take much time to do, but it could save a lot of time if the need for information arises due to unexpected circumstances.

Make a note of your attorney's and accountant's names and write down their addresses, phone numbers, fax numbers, and e-mail addresses. Next list the same information for your bank, including the name of the representative you deal with most. Now put down the name and contact information for the executor of your estate. If you are a member of a synagogue or church, write down the address and phone number, along with the name of the rabbi or minister and the head of the congregation.

Gather your insurance data and record the agent and agency names and contact information for your life, health, homeowner's, car, and disability insurance. Put down the policy numbers and expiration dates of each policy, plus where the policies are located. If you have any additional insurance such as an umbrella policy, list it here with the appropriate contact information.

Now note your primary physician's name, address, phone, and fax numbers and any specialists you see regularly. Record the name of the nearest hospital and ambulance service. Write down the name and address of the company you work for and contact information for your immediate supervisor.

Put the finished list in your active home files and give a copy to each of your adult children and a close friend or trusted relative.

Information at Your Fingertips

Several types of personal and financial information are best filed at home, where they can be easily accessed. These include your educational records, such as diplomas and transcripts, and your employment history, including dates, locations, and references for each job you held. If you have a resume listing professional accomplishments and memberships in industry organizations, file it with your employment records.

In addition, keep all your family medical records together in this file. This is the place to list immunizations, major illnesses, surgeries, physicians' names and addresses, and hospital information. While the originals of your family's birth and death certificates should be kept in the safe-deposit box, place copies of these records here in your personal files.

Your financial records in this active home file should include unpaid bills and bank and brokerage statements, along with credit card information. You should have a sheet listing all your credit cards, their numbers and expiration dates, and the number to call if they are lost or stolen. Store the last five years of cancelled checks here also, along with mortgage information and data about other loans. File these together with tax receipts, working papers, and tax returns from the last five years.

You can make files for each category or store related items together. For example, when organizing your insurance policies, gather your car, homeowner's, life, medical, and disability papers together and place them in this file. Make a place for major appliance manuals and warrantee information, marking the date and place of each purchase. Keep the receipts so you can get help if anything goes wrong. In addition, make a file for your home improvement records and receipts.

Files that you keep in home storage should include all tax returns and cancelled checks that are older than five years and proof that major debts have been repaid. If you owned a house previously, keep the home improvement records there.

All About Life Insurance

While we all hope for long and healthy lives, no one, of course, can insure the future; the closest we can come is to purchase life insurance, an investment we make to try to protect our family in case we are no longer able to do so ourselves. But who should have life insurance? And what kind? And for how much? All these are questions that have different answers at different times of our lives, and as we age and our children leave home we need to reassess the type and size of coverage that is right for us.

Many financial experts insist that life insurance is nothing more than a form of legalized gambling. The insurance company bets you will die within the year; you bet you won't. Your insurance premium is your stake. If you die, you win, and your insurance company must pay your beneficiary. If you don't die, the insurance company wins, and you place a bet for another year. The fact is life insurance companies make most of their money by investing the bets or premiums you pay them, so they are eager to bring in as many as possible and make them as high as they can. But how much you pay for the premium is less important that what you get for it.

Whether or not you can obtain adequate coverage for your needs depends on many factors, including your employer, your personal health, and the laws of the state in which you live. In ideal circumstances, the amount of life insurance you should buy would allow your spouse and children to continue living the way they live now. But it is never easy to translate this goal into dollars and cents. Some financial planners suggest that your coverage range between four and six times your income, but this depends on the value of your other assets and the age of your family. Families with young children, for example, are generally encouraged to purchase higher coverage, but as your children go off to college and grow closer to self-sufficiency, the amount of insurance you need is said to drop.

Whether you buy life insurance through an agent, directly from a savings bank, or through a group policy, you will face a stunning array of choices that can seem unnecessarily complex. Even comparing the actual costs of two policies of the same kind can be confusing. Often the true costs are indistinct because of differences in dividend payments, premium schedules, and the accrual of cash value.

Many sources of help exist, however. If you choose to use an insurance agent, for example, find one who has passed the rigorous series of exams that make him or her a Chartered Life Underwriter. This designation indicates a high level of education and professionalism. Two helpful publications that publish unbiased evaluations of insurance companies on a regular basis are *Consumer Reports* and *Best's Insurance Reports*. Check in your public library or online to find out how they rate the insurance companies that are of interest to you. You can also ask your state insurance commission about specific companies and their practices. This watchdog group monitors consumer complaints and regulates the insurance industry in each state so they know when a company develops practices you might find unacceptable.

The Nuts and Bolts of Making a Will

The single most important item in insuring the financial future of your children is a comprehensive, valid, and properly executed will. Yet two out of every three American adults do not have one. This effectively allows a probate judge to divide up their property according to the laws of the state. Without a will the court must follow the exact letter of the law, despite what may seem like impersonal and inflexible directives and the ensuing emotional and financial consequences to your family.

No one consciously wants to shortchange their family, of course, but the emotional issues surrounding wills can be so difficult to grapple with that people choose to ignore them instead. If you do not yet have an attorney, making a plan to create a will is a good way to find one. If you do have one, set up a meeting to draft a will or reevaluate your current one if it is more than five years old.

There are several standard steps to take in making a will. First, you should think about who you would like to name as executor. This is the person who will make sure your debts are paid and your property is distributed the way you want it. Choose a person who is responsible, respected by your family, and not much older than you. Without a named executor the probate court will appoint an administrator who will collect a hefty fee for his or her services.

Next, you should think of specific gifts you might want to leave to certain members of your family. You might want to give a beloved piece of jewelry or set of heirloom furniture to a son or daughter who has always particularly admired it. Or perhaps you would like to help a cousin start a nest egg with a specific amount of money or a percentage of the estate.

When your children were younger, it was necessary to name a guardian for them in your will. But in most states once they turn eighteen this is no longer the case. If you live in one of the few states that require a guardian until age twenty-one, however, check with your attorney about how to proceed.

Although it is bound to be difficult to discuss, consider whether you want your children to inherit your property equally. One may have special needs that you want to fulfill. Another may be in a vastly different income bracket from his or her siblings. The residuary estate—all the property that is not specifically mentioned anywhere else in the will—will be divided among your heirs as you specify.

Don't worry about locking yourself in; you can always change your mind and rewrite your will or add a codicil, the Latin word for "little will" that is the term for a written amendment. It is a good idea to

---

QUIZ: HOW THOROUGH IS YOUR ESTATE PLANNING?

To make sure you have provided for your children's security as well as possible, answer each of the following questions and give yourself five points for each "yes" answer. After you are finished, check the end of the quiz to see what your score means.

1. I have made a clear calculation of my net worth, including cash on hand, checking and savings accounts, CDs, mutual funds, stocks, bonds, life insurance, jewelry and furs, cars and real estate, and subtracted liabilities, including the balances of mortgages and other loans, credit card balances, and owed taxes.
2. I have decided how I want to distribute my assets.
3. I know what my federal and state tax bill will be this year.
4. I have considered whether to set up a trust to avoid taxes.
5. I have named an executor for my will.
6. I have written a letter of instruction describing my final wishes, and my family knows my plans.
7. I have created a durable power of attorney.
8. My will has been written, approved, witnessed, and signed.
9. My will is safely stored with my attorney, with a copy in my files.
10. I have executed a living will.

If you scored between forty and fifty points, you should consider your family well covered. Nevertheless, estate planning is an area of such importance that those scoring between forty and forty-five points might want to take steps to move up to fifty points, a perfect score. If you scored thirty to thirty-five points, you are on your way but not there yet. Review your plans and take action. Below thirty points indicates a family in need of legal and financial advice. Don't hesitate in seeking it.

reevaluate your will if there is a major change in federal estate or tax laws, in your financial status, or in the health care needs of a family member.

Remember to review and update your will periodically—at least every five years—to allow for changed circumstances. Today your children might be in college, but as every parent knows they were in diapers only yesterday and are bound to produce grandchildren before tomorrow is even over.

Tips on Tackling Probate

Probate court supervises the distribution of your property whether you have a will or not. No one likes probate—it takes time and costs money. How much of each depends on how intricate the will is, how valuable the estate is, and how many beneficiaries there are. You can minimize the effects of probate and maximize your children's inheritance if you plan ahead, working out various legal ways to pass specific amounts of property outside your will.

The first way to do this is through joint property ownership. If you and your spouse and/or child have a joint tenancy with the right of survivorship, the property you own automatically goes to your co-owner or owners, avoiding probate altogether. Written documentation is necessary for joint tenancy, and both names must be on the title or deed of the property in question, be it a car, a house, a mutual fund account, or an appraised collection of jewelry.

Another effective way to avoid probate is to transfer money through gifts. These are limited in dollar amount, but using the system wisely will allow you to give away a substantial amount of money tax free to any number of individuals. You must remember, however, that once you surpass the allowable amount, any money you give will be subject to gift taxes, which are charged to you, the giver, not the recipient. One effective use of the gift allowance is to employ it to lower the overall value of your estate so it is not large enough to be subject to federal estate taxes.

You can also pass funds outside of probate through your insurance benefits. For example, benefits from a life insurance policy made payable to your estate would be probated, but this is not so if an individual is named as the beneficiary.

The final method is to set up a trust, which works like a corporation and legally owns the property transferred to it. A trust is a complicated entity, owned by its beneficiaries but managed by its trustees and liable for taxes if it earns more than a specific amount of income each year. Trusts vary from the testamentary kind, which are created by your will to protect your children's inheritance, to living trusts, which you set up while you are alive and are not part of your will. In either case, trusts are complex legal entities that require an attorney or estate planner to set up and administer.

PART V

Making Your Home Yours Again

Chapter
Seventeen

NEW WAYS TO FEATHER
THE NEST

It seems you hear about it every other day, another couple pulling up stakes and moving to Florida or Arizona or trading their house for an apartment in the city. But you've always felt so rooted in your home, almost as though you were planted in the garden along with the rhododendrons and the rose bushes. You could never leave the kitchen you designed yourself, with every electrical outlet placed just where you wanted it, every floor tile set in the direction you mapped out for the contractor.

Or could you? Just for fun you flip through the real estate section in the Sunday paper, scanning the ads for property in your neighborhood. There have been times when you wondered if you would someday want to trade in your colonial for a ranch house, with no stairs to aggravate your knees on rainy days. Or move to one of those new, easy-care condos on the golf course just a little way out of town. But certainly not now. Your identity is here. Your security is here.

But it's more than that, you know. You have spent so many seasons checking the foundation walls and the basement windows, making sure the insulation and the roof tiles and the gutters and leaders were all in working order. You have not only protected your investment, but worked hard to make it worth even more. Didn't you supervise the new boiler installation last spring and the extension of the gas line to the outdoor barbecue grill just this summer?

Yet when you check the prices in the newspaper, you see that a house like yours on a street like the one you live on just sold for an astonishingly high price. Maybe you should consider what you could do with all that cash, if you were to sell. Maybe you shouldn't be so, well, sentimental, especially now when money is more of an issue than ever with the sky-high college tuition bills you have to pay.

You go to your desk in the den to get a pad and pencil, but as you step inside the room your eyes won't seem to move past the tiny lines on the doorframe, the marks you made periodically in indelible ink to measure your kids' growth. Oh, for how many years did you celebrate and worry and cheer over those lines? It is hard to count; it feels like forever.

How can you even consider leaving this house now, you wonder, when you can't even bring yourself to paint the doorframe. How can you ever consider it?

Balancing Dollars, Desires, and Housing Options

Real estate experts say that most people can safely afford to spend 35 percent of their gross income on housing. This includes not only mortgage and taxes, but also insurance, heating, maintenance, and repairs. Another way to express this safety range is to say that monthly home costs should not exceed one-and-a-half weeks of a family's take-home pay. Either way you look at it, however, once college tuition bills kick in and the need to provide space for three, four, or five diminishes, some financial planners recommend moving to smaller, less expensive quarters.

Is this right for you? Probably no decision is more personal or more deserving of a close evaluation than this one, as every family member will be affected by a move, each in his or her own way. Indeed, your home is most likely your largest long-term investment, and how you use it, change it, leverage it, or trade it has lasting implications for your family's emotional and financial future.

Owning and maintaining a home is, of course, a complicated, multifaceted and somewhat daunting experience at any age, but in some ways it grows more complex as we age. For an increasing number of people whose children have grown up and left home, a favored strategy is to become renters. About 35 percent of Americans prefer not to buy a home and rent instead.

People who choose to live this way believe there are many advantages to renting. It gives them more mobility while also allowing them to invest their money elsewhere. It means never having to worry about declining property values in their neighborhood, and absolves them of a level of community involvement that can demand effort and commitment they no longer want to make.

But for others the emotional benefits of owning property continue to outweigh the advantages of renting. While staying in the housing market is certainly not without its attendant risks, statistics solidly show that the median price of single-family homes tends to rise significantly each year. And although paying off a mortgage each month can drain the financial coffers, it is in effect a form of compulsory savings, as you are building assets toward retirement each time you pay off a portion of the principal.

Consider a Condo or Co-Op

Many couples who move out of their prime child-rearing years but still want to own their own home choose to purchase a cooperative or condominium in an apartment building, garden apartment complex, or attached townhouse community. These choices require less maintenance than owning a house, since paid personnel do the repairs and the gardening and there are often added amenities like tennis courts, game rooms, and pools. But they also impose restrictions, often disallowing pets or small children to live on the property and limiting structural changes you may want to make to your living space.

Co-ops and condos can be excellent investments, just like single-family houses, but they differ from each other in significant ways. The down payment for a co-op is likely to be far lower than for a comparable condo, for example, while the maintenance fee can be more than twice as high. Co-op owners often find it more difficult to sell their unit, as potential buyers must be approved by the co-op board. As the owner of a condo, on the other hand, it is entirely up to you to decide whether to sell or lease your unit and to whom.

Co-op owners have the benefits of deducting their mortgage interest payments and property taxes from their income tax, but condo owners do not. However, a significant drawback to owning a co-op is that if another owner is delinquent on his or her payments, for example, or if one or more units remain sold, the rest of the co-op owners will be required to pay for these expenses. In both cases, it is important to make sure monthly maintenance fees do not exceed officially projected costs.

A Move or a Makeover?

While financial considerations are primary in whether or not a move is a wise decision, people are often propelled into relocating for more than just monetary reasons. There are often compelling personal factors as well. Some parents whose children have left home for college find that although they still love their living space, they no longer feel at home in the neighborhood.

This can happen for many reasons, and most of them can be best understood by tracing back to the reasons you moved to the community in the first place. If you chose your area for its excellent public schools, for example, and all your children have graduated, it may be that you are no longer willing to pay the high property taxes that usually accompany highly developed school systems. If that is the case, you are likely to be able to trade in your house for one with more square footage and larger property in a community with a lower-rated school system.

Perhaps you have changed jobs since you purchased your last house and now want to be closer to your work or are tired of a long commute. Better access to your office can mean additional hours for leisure activities and more time at home.

City Lights Versus Suburban Safety

Another factor to evaluate is the proximity of your home to a city. If you moved to the suburbs when your children were young, you might not have cared about developments in the theater, music, and art worlds. How important was it to you to try out new restaurants in the city? How often did you frequent new cabarets, comedy clubs, or coffee-houses?

If you had little energy for nighttime entertainment in your prime parenting years, you were like most parents of young children. And if you want to enjoy the stimulation of the city now that your kids have left home, you are like most parents once again. Often this desire engenders interest in a move to a rental or co-op apartment in the city.

What about other amenities, like the parks, libraries, and shopping centers in your community? Do they matter to you in the same ways and to the same degree that they did while your major activity was being a parent? If you want to pursue an intellectual interest, for example, does your local library contain material on the level you need? Can you shop in your area for the items that suit your lifestyle now? If you don't want to continue relying on a car, is the public transportation system adequate to take you to the places that interest you?

All these factors go into making a decision about where to live. For many couples the answer is clear-cut, for others it is hazy at first and only comes into focus as the discussion ensues. But the truth is that either decision is likely to involve change, because even those couples who decide to stay put in their family home will find that life without children significantly alters the way their household functions. Some will find they want to redecorate or even reconfigure their living space, but even those who don't will find that new patterns of living create many welcome opportunities to add new levels of beauty, serenity, and excitement to their homes.

The Heart of the Matter

For parents who decide this is not a time to make a move and opt to stay where they are, there are two schools of thought about how best to adapt a family home to a space just right for a couple. One advocates preserving the family atmosphere as much as possible by replacing what the last departing child took away and making only minor changes to the rest; the other proposes reevaluating the needs and wishes of the couple and redesigning the space to accommodate their new way of life.

Both have their merits, of course. On the preservation side, parents who believe it is important to keep a child's room and primary living areas exactly as they always were feel this way for a variety of reasons. They believe this offers security and support while the child is away and comfort and familiarity when he or she comes home on vacations. If a calendar was removed from a wall at home and installed in the child's new quarters, it is replaced with another one. Lamps, shades, computers, wall hangings, posters, even desk items that left along with their owner leave empty spaces that must be filled in kind. Shared family space in a den or playroom area is not significantly altered either, leaving it ready for the child to use upon returning home, and most likely helping parents feel their offspring is not really gone yet.

This option is certainly not for everyone, but for parents who may feel left behind by their last child's departure and who need some time to catch up, it can provide just the measure of comfort they require to become more able to accept the sometimes startling reality of their child's new life in college. And it has other benefits too: A student coming home for vacation will not have to cope with feeling replaced, pushed out, or pushed aside. A comfortable bed, much-needed privacy, and the safe familiarity of childhood surroundings can offer a sensitive child the security he or she needs to go back to the more challenging hurly-burly world of college when the vacation is over.

Much of the decision of whether to preserve the old or concentrate on creating the new is based on the relationship between the parents and child, both spoken and unspoken, and the kind of marriage that the parents have created for themselves. Sooner or later, however, even parents who choose this conservative approach will find their own needs pushing to the forefront, compelling them to make changes in their home that reflect their altered lives.

Take an Inventory of Your Living Space

As soon as you and your spouse can find a block of time, plan a leisurely walk through your house, from top to bottom, and examine it through new eyes. Your main task is to go from room to room, look at what the space has been used for all along and consider how you might use it now. Let your imagination loose! Take along a clipboard or a legal pad and pen and take an inventory of what you see.

This is not as simple as it seems. Over the years it is likely that many wishes and dreams were squelched because of lack of space in which to achieve them. Did you envision a sewing room when you first bought your house or apartment, but needed the extra bedroom for

HOME IMPROVEMENT RESOURCES

Whether you want to convert a significant amount of space in your home or just update a small area, you want to make sure you do it right. Maybe you have the skill and patience to handle the project yourself, or perhaps you need to hire an expert to do the job. Either way, these books will help you plan and execute the job to add value and comfort to your home.

Converting Basements, Garages and Attics, by R. Dodge Woodson, published by Sterling Publishing Co., 1993. Learn the basics of taking unused space and turning it into beautiful living areas. Step-by-step instructions show you how to visualize, design, and increase your square footage without adding an inch of space.

Don't Move—Improve! by Katie and Gene Hamilton, published by Henry Holt Books, 1992. Avoid the expense, frustration, and disruption of moving by enhancing your current home with tried-and-true remodeling projects and techniques, carefully detailed in this useful book. Tips and tricks to make the work easier are included throughout.

Better Homes and Gardens New Remodeling Book, published by Meredith Co., 1998. Like paying college tuition for your kids, remodeling your house is a major investment that requires planning, perseverance, and the ability to stick to a budget. Use the expertise of architects, contractors, and financial experts in this helpful guide to put your home through a dramatic transformation.

Reviving Old Houses, by Alan Dan Orme, published by Garden Way Publishing Co., 1989. Old and new techniques developed by a professional who finds beauty and romance in giving new life to old houses and believes you can do the same. Save money on building materials, learn how to weatherize, restore masonry, rebuild chimneys, and renovate interiors while providing upgraded living space for your family.

the baby on the way? Would you have liked to set up an art studio in the attic but never had the money to put in a roof window? Would you run ballet classes in the basement if you could only install a set of mirrors and a barre?

The list of possibilities is unlimited. If you found a way to make space for an office, for example, would you tutor neighborhood kids in math or advise high school seniors on how to apply to college? Do you have a space you would like to use for an exercise room, someplace larger than the closet in which you now house your stationary bike and collapsible treadmill? Have you always had a piano but secretly wish to use that corner for a harp? Have you ever wanted a pool table?

Many of your answers will depend on whether you moved into the house with or without children. If you bought your home as a couple, you may have had in mind to fill the bedrooms with children. But before they became a reality, what did you use those rooms for? Was one bedroom an office? Was another a library? If you can envision how the space was used before you had children, it will be far easier to find new, good uses for it now.

If you moved into the house with your family already up and running and have never imagined the place without children, it will be a little harder. But no matter where you lived before the kids were born, you and your spouse most likely spent some time developing your own goals and wishes and dreams. What were they? How did you implement them? How can you make space for them now?

New Treasures in Old Houses

Think about your garage, for example. Do you use it for your car? Most people don't. Instead, they use it to store a variety of gardening equipment, old toys, outdoor chairs, and other semiuseful paraphernalia. Certainly storage is fine, but keeping old stuff takes up room, which takes away that room from new activities that might interest us if we had the chance to try them out.

Often we don't even know what those activities are. It is empty space that makes us daydream, and daydreams often grow into concrete ideas. Many legitimate enterprises have their humble origins in

HOW TO CHOOSE AND USE A CONTRACTOR

While you are debating whether to spend money on a renovation project, consider that the National Association of Realtors maintains that nearly all improvements aid in the resale value of your home, often by far more than your actual expense. The industry trade group does recommend, however, that before you remodel you determine the cost of homes in your area and add no more value to your own house than 20 percent above the highest priced home. This is to avoid owning a house that will be overpriced for its community, as that would make it difficult to sell.

Make a sketch of what you want and start looking for a contractor who is both honest and skilled and has a degree of business savvy. You don't want someone who will disappear after receiving the first payment or who will remove the cabinets in your kitchen but fail to appear the next day to install the new ones. Nor do you want an unscrupulous contractor who will use inferior materials or skip steps in the plans. Check around and get personal recommendations from friends and neighbors or ask an architect in your area. Make sure that all recommended contractors are licensed and bonded.

The rule of thumb is to ask three contractors to bid on the job. In evaluating the bids, experts recommend taking the middle one. The reasoning is that the highest is suspected of having built in too high a profit margin and the lowest might cut corners.

It is customary to pay 15 percent of the total dollar amount of the project when you sign the contract. For the rest of the work, create a payment schedule with pay periods for specific portions of the job that have been completed to your satisfaction, and do not allow yourself to be convinced to pay the next installment in advance. Plan to retain 25 percent of the cost of the project for the final payment to guarantee that the contractor will finish the job. Finally, keep accurate records of your expenses. Capital improvements can be added to the price of your home when you sell it to lower your capital gain.

garages: rock bands have been born and nurtured to maturity there; scientists who were banished from the main house have found refuge and inspiration; inventors who simply needed a place to tinker have made their discoveries there.

Try looking at the upstairs bedrooms from your new perspective. Are these rooms repositories for old memories? If they are and you want to preserve them, can they at least be consolidated? Can all the scrapbooks, baseball cards, and old valentines make it into one room, leaving another free for a creative endeavor of some sort?

Once you have done your inventory, look over your notes and see how you can work your new ideas into your life. Some of them you will be able to implement right away, as soon as you clear up the clutter and install a new desk or easel or computer. Getting started on these projects as soon as possible is guaranteed to lift your spirits and give life a new dimension. Others will require some major renovations. For these you will need a remodeling plan and most likely a contractor. Beginning the work is the first step toward reclaiming your space and making your home and your life your own again.

Chapter Eighteen

A SECOND CHANCE AT LIVING WELL

Dinner out with friends used to be your favorite Saturday night activity. But this weekend, as you sip your margarita in the restaurant lounge before heading for your table, you find yourself looking around at all the other diners, wondering if they are having a better time than you.

It's not that the conversation isn't as quick and witty as usual, or that your friends aren't interested in your life. You've gone out with these two other couples so many times over the years that you have a storehouse of shared experiences to laugh over, and new ideas are flowing among you as easily as ever tonight. Yet even as you take part in the exchange, you are aware of a brittle quality to your voice, a sense of remoteness in your attitude, as though you somehow feel you don't belong.

During the meal you find yourself participating less and watching more. Somehow everything seems too lavish tonight, almost overdone. The flowers needn't be so showy, you find yourself thinking. The music is so loud; why do we need a three-piece band in this small place when a simple piano player would do just fine? And the wine is too expensive. Well, maybe not for everyone, but certainly for you.

Perhaps that's at the bottom of your discontent, you think now, spending so much for an evening out, with tuition looming over you and college expenses popping up everywhere you look. Bills, bills,

bills! You can't seem to go anywhere without them following you, dogging your footsteps no matter what you do.

You excuse yourself and walk out onto the terrace, breathing in the cold air with sharp relief. Now that you have the time for fancy nights out on the town, you're not enjoying them, not when you're spending money you'd really rather use to catch up on everything you owe. There has to be at least a million ways to have a good time without spending an arm and a leg. But you've always gone out this way with these friends. How are you going to figure out a new way to do it?

Spend Less Without Sacrificing Your Lifestyle

For many couples, paying college tuition on top of keeping up with all the other expenses of running a complex household can create a burden of unexpected proportions. Despite their best estimates, the actual costs of supporting a child in college often run considerably higher than planned. Not everyone factors in the big bite taken out of a budget by set-up costs, for example, or the ongoing nibbles of a child's active social life. Sure, you've protected your income and you've done well with your investments. But you haven't really examined your spending to see where you could economize.

Like most parents, however, you've probably developed a built-in proclivity for flexible planning over the years, and sooner or later you're likely to take a good, long look at your lifestyle and see what needs to be changed. You don't want to drain your resources, both financial and emotional, but you want to continue living well. So how do you get started? Here are some simple steps you can take right now to get going on the right path.

First, take a look at your utility bills. Do you want to find out how to lower them? Consider requesting an energy audit. This is one of the best services your utility company offers. All you have to do is ask, and your local utility company will send a qualified conservation expert to your house to perform a complete energy inspection at no charge. Your furnace will be checked to see if it is energy efficient. Your windows will be inspected for proper caulking and weather stripping. Your air conditioners will be evaluated to determine whether they are the right size for your needs. When the review is done, you will be sent a specifically tailored recommendation outlining the energy-saving measures that will work in your home, what they cost, and how much they will save on your monthly bill.

Next, examine your shopping habits. When purchasing big-ticket items like DVD players, TVs, and refrigerators, for example, are you tempted to buy the service contract? Don't. You don't need it, and it can add up to 10 percent to the purchase price. Most electronics that break down do so in the first year, during which the item will be covered by a warranty anyway.

You can also save by evaluating where you put your cash. Move money in your checking account to higher interest-bearing accounts like mutual funds or money market accounts, keeping only the minimum in a bank checking account to cover immediate expenses and allow you to make necessary payments. In addition, look over your insurance bills and find out if you can lower your premiums by raising the deductibles.

Are you paying for services you can get for free elsewhere? Look over the terms of your credit card and see if one is available at a competitive bank for no annual fee. Pay off your credit card debt even it means you have to borrow the money elsewhere, as the interest rate will be lower and you will still come out ahead. And if you get a tax refund this year, don't spend it! Put it in savings or a safe investment.

QUIZ: DO YOU KNOW HOW TO UTILIZE YOUR UTILITIES?

According to the U.S. Department of Energy, for every dollar you spend on gas, oil, electricity, and water, the largest share—46 cents—goes toward heating and cooling your house. Even if you are determined to keep the thermostat at a comfortable level during both summer and winter, you can take steps to save energy and lower your utility costs. Take this quiz to find out if you know what to do. Answer true or false for each of the following statements and then check your score at the end.

1. A well-insulated house with a two-by-two-foot hole in its side loses the same amount of heat as a house with average insulation. True _____ False _____
2. If you install storm windows, fireplace dampers, and weather

stripping in your house, you will pay up to 20 percent less to heat it than before. True _____ False _____

3. More than half of the energy you buy to heat a house escapes through the ceilings, walls, and floors. True _____ False _____

4. Insulating your attic will enable you to save 30 percent off your heating bill. True _____ False _____

5. Giving your furnace a tune-up will increase its energy efficiency by 5 percent. True _____ False _____

6. Installing a humidifier on your furnace will enable you to lower the thermostat several degrees and still feel comfortable. True _____ False _____

7. Raising the temperature two degrees on your thermostat in the summer can cut cooling costs by 5 percent. Lowering the thermostat by the same number of degrees in winter cuts heating costs by the same amount. True _____ False _____

8. A heat pump, installed outside the house, can provide both heating and air-conditioning and reduce bills by as much as 40 percent. True _____ False _____

9. Windows permit ten times more heat to escape from your house than walls. True _____ False _____

10. When purchasing replacement windows, buy the ones with the highest "R" value. True _____ False _____

Answers: 1—True. 2—False. (Good news: you will save even more, paying 30 percent less, not 20.) 3—True. 4—True. 5—True. 6—True. 7—False. (You save 5 percent for every degree you lower your thermostat, not every two degrees.) 8—True. 9—False. (Windows permit even more heat—twelve times as much—to escape from your house.) 10—True.

Setting Priorities for Entertainment

We all need to relax, but we don't necessarily need to pay premium prices to do so. Check out your TV-watching habits and see if you really need the high-priced cable package. How often to you actually watch HBO? Less than when your kids were still at home? How much could you save every month if you went back to basic cable, especially if you had it on only one TV, or no cable at all?

If eating out is an important priority, go out for lunch instead of dinner. The savings are considerable. If you must meet your friends in the evening, suggest coffee and dessert instead of a full meal. You will be surprised at how festive it is to eat a simple meal at home and then join others at a fun place for dessert.

You can save money on your entertainment budget if you go to film festivals at local colleges instead of to movie theaters. Museums and libraries show feature films too, at low cost or for free. And you can always borrow videos from the library instead of renting them from the local video store. Likewise, you do not have to miss important sporting events just because you don't want to pay for seats at the arena. Enjoy them with other fans at a sports bar or restaurant in your neighborhood.

Most of us don't want to live without music, but if you balk at spending $100 for orchestra seats at a concert hall, look for free outdoor classical or folk concerts in neighborhood parks in the summer or buy half-price tickets for same-day showings at special ticket booths. Secondhand CDs, cassette tapes, and record albums are cheap and plentiful at library sales and summertime garage sales. You might also consider trading music with friends to vary your collection and improve theirs at the same time.

What about vacations? It's important to change your routine and see new places, but are you willing to live a little closer to nature than usual? If so, try camping. You don't have to sleep in a tent—staying in a cabin with kitchen facilities is the most inexpensive way to travel and can provide a very romantic interlude for a couple newly freed from the work of caring for teenagers, especially if your a trip goes through the national parks or to the seashore.

If you want to take a more traditional vacation and stay in hotels, you can still carry an ice chest and eat a simple breakfast in your room, then lunch at picnic areas with homemade sandwiches. Dinner out at night will be more of a treat this way, and the money you save will be significant. Whenever possible, plan a driving vacation instead of flying and renting a car to keep costs considerably lower.

How to Get off the More-Is-Better Treadmill

Did you read all the magazines you subscribed to this past year? Do you want to keep getting them all, or are some beyond your interests now? Cancel all those you no longer read regularly, and use your public library to keep up with them if you want to remain current. You can also take advantage of free trial offers and then cancel when the free part runs out. Keep your hand in many publications for a small cost by setting up a magazine exchange club with friends.

You may have club memberships that you no longer need now that your children are not at home anymore. Country clubs, golf clubs, and health clubs may have been important last year, but perhaps your life has changed and the expense is no longer worthwhile. Take a look at the costs and see how often you think you will use the club this year. Is there an inexpensive alternative? Could you use the gym at the local Y? Are there newly built pools, tennis courts, or golf courses in your community that offer lower fees? Have you passed a certain age that would entitle you to a lower-cost membership? Will fees go down if you go off the family plan and into a couples or a singles membership?

We all spend a surprisingly large amount of money on the upkeep of our homes, and if you are serious about spending less you might try six months without your housecleaning service and your landscape gardener. Learning how to do your own repairs by borrowing books from the fix-it-yourself section of the library is a great money-saver too.

While you are at it, if you can learn how to paint, plaster, and wallpaper, you will have gained precious skills that can save you considerable amounts of money. Not everyone can be an artist or an craftsperson, of course, but we can all mow the lawn, maintain the driveway, and hammer down loose nails in the deck. If you don't know how, ask a neighbor. Borrow tools at first, but plan to invest the money to buy your own.

When in Doubt, Simplify

Spending less doesn't have to mean working harder, but when it does, make sure you pamper yourself in some way to sweeten the experience of expending extra effort. The key to success is not to do it too often. For example, if you feel it's a treat to get an expensive hair styling, manicure, or exotic spa treatment, by all means do so. If you

HOW MUCH IS ENOUGH? COMMENTS FROM THE EXPERTS

"The 'don't save more, earn more' philosophy is a very one-sided approach. . . . There is a point at which the quality of life and the standard of living depart, where earning more results in a personal cost and erodes the quality of life."

—*Amy Dacyczyn, editor,* The Tightwad Gazette, *a monthly newsletter promoting thrift as an alternative lifestyle*

"Living simply is about eliminating the excess, so you will be free to discover who you really are. By simplifying you will save time and money, gain control of your possessions, save energy and focus on what is important. It is the perfect antidote for a stressful life."

—*Cris Evatt and Connie Cox, coauthors,* Thirty Days to a Simpler Life

"Choose your existence. Don't sail through life on automatic pilot. Design your life to coincide with your ideals."

—*Janet Lurhs, editor of* Simple Living: The Journal of Voluntary Simplicity, *a quarterly newsletter*

want to meet friends at a favorite club at the end of the work week, certainly make some plans. Just don't do it every week.

Save the visits for special occasions, or reward yourself at regularly spaced intervals so you can really look forward to them. Cutting back and cutting out do not have to mean eliminating luxury forever; it just means establishing limits and keeping a tight reign on spending, or finding less expensive alternatives.

Don't forget old-fashioned fun, the kind that has been out of style for a generation or two but can still be remembered and savored by older people who grew up in a less affluent time and had to create their own entertainment. Try talking to relatives who recall standing around the piano and singing family favorites, playing board games, even as adults, or reading to each other.

The major difference between these activities and the popular fun pastimes of today is not only the cost but, more importantly, the intimacy. Playing croquet or badminton, sharing picnics and cookouts, or walking through the zoo holding hands can't be compared to watching TV or playing video games for the personal contact and closeness they engender. Few people today still play charades or work on jigsaw puzzles together, but you can revive these traditions in your home.

Passive fun simply does not engage the mind the way active entertainment does. It costs nothing but creative effort to arrange a neighborhood scavenger hunt for a group of friends, for example, and after a night of homemade mayhem, it could be you will spend your next weekend together writing and producing a play, complete with script, costumes, and a small audience of neighbors.

Cooking for Two

Your food budget is a natural place to find easy and plentiful ways to save money, not only by learning how to economize on ingredients and food preparation methods, but by learning how to eat more healthfully and cut down on work time. Now is a perfectly natural time for you to learn these techniques, since you are no longer cooking for your college-age child and will have to adapt to a new regimen in any case.

It is not unreasonable to expect that you could reduce your expenditures to a third or even a quarter of what you have spent in the past, even above and beyond the money you will save by no longer feeding your teenager. This can provide you with substantial savings that you will be happy to apply elsewhere, especially if it means being able to offer your child an extra dinner out now and then as a break from the college dining hall.

Many of us have become so used to convenience in the kitchen that we tend to think of the four food groups as microwavable, freeze-dried, canned, and shrink-wrapped. We spend money on timesaving products without thinking about the cost and, sadly, often we sacrifice nutrition too. We buy vegetables precut and frozen, cheese already grated, meats presliced, and cake batter already mixed without considering that everything bottled, dehydrated, and prepackaged is sold at an additional cost because of the extra effort involved in its production. In exchange, we lose not only money but vitamins, minerals, fiber, and freshness.

Most of us won't consider cooking everything from scratch. We want meals that are economical and nutritionally sound, but considering the other demands on our time we are limited in what we can do. The answer is eating more simply.

For example, the simplest cooking for people who like meat as the center of an entrée is to rely primarily on roasts. You can cook a big turkey, roast beef, ham, or chicken on the weekend and provide meals in a most economical way for the entire week. When the cooking is done, a half hour or so should be enough to take the meat off the bones, wrap it in meal-size portions and freeze it.

If you start by making two roasts the first week and then a different one each week after that, you will have a nice variety of meat and poultry in the freezer from which to choose. You can thaw each night's dinner in the microwave and then turn it into a stir-fry or add a special sauce and serve over freshly cooked pasta. Toss a salad and you have a simple, nutritious meal in a short time.

You can make this type of dinner even more special by serving it with homemade bread, baked on an evening home or on a weekend morning. It takes time to bake bread, of course, but not as much time as you think if you have one of the new varieties of bread machines. The investment you must make to buy it will come back to you tenfold as you enjoy the homey aroma of bread baking in your kitchen and the warm sense of abundance provided by even the simplest bread. And a loaf of freshly baked bread specially wrapped and sent to a child away at college is also an incredibly nice way to provide a taste of home across the miles.

Dollars in Your Shopping Cart

How do you shop for food? Do you plan your menus and go to the supermarket once a week or visit the grocery store daily for fresh produce? Do you do a major shopping trip once a month, stock your freezer, and purchase perishables when you need them?

No matter which style of shopping you use, it's most economical to make a plan and follow it. You are less likely to fall prey to impulse buying if you go into the store with a list you know you can stick to. That means not shopping when you are hungry, for example, or at the end of the day when you are so tired you will pick items off a promi-nent display rather than hunt for the lower-priced brands that are pur-posefully harder to find.

Marketing experts know what they are doing—that's why they have their jobs. So stick to your list and your budget, and don't go shop-ping with family members who can't.

Some communities have discount warehouse stores, where you can often find great savings if you buy in bulk. If this is available to you, buy your staples once a month and purchase flour and sugar, for example, in twenty-five- to fifty-pound bags. If you can't store it con-veniently, divide it up and share it among a group of friends. Buying as a team will also reduce the number of shopping trips you have to make.

Make sure you build in enough time on your trips to comparison shop. Compare brands and sizes for economy. Check out ingredients to make sure you are getting maximum nutrition and a minimum of preservatives and other chemicals in your food. Take along a calcula-tor and work out price-to-size ratios. You will be surprised to see that buying the largest package is not always the most economical way to shop.

Stores often place their cheapest brands on the highest and lowest shelves, so make sure you look there to see how the items compare in price. Distributors pay a premium to have their wares displayed on the shelves at eye level, and they pass on those costs to you. Keep an open mind and try out store brands and generic products, which are always a little bit less costly. Some may not work, but others will.

You will make your shopping far more effective if you learn to think like a marketer. Don't count on using coupons to save money, for ex-ample. Why? Most coupons are designed to get you to try new items, mostly prepared items and convenience foods. Do take advantage of sales, however. Always pick up a flyer when you enter the store and see what the specials are. Three cans of tomato paste for the price of two? Pick up six, if you have room to store them.

Another way to save money is to buy only food products at the gro-cery store. Purchase shampoo and toothpaste at the pharmacy, laun-dry detergent and cleaning tools at the hardware store. Don't pay more for convenience if you can take the time to shop for better prices elsewhere.

Chapter
Nineteen

HEALTH, FITNESS, AND LONGEVITY

The rain is whipping at your windshield as you steer down the highway at a slow but steady pace, wishing you'd left a little earlier so you wouldn't be driving at night. But the visit to your child's college for the lacrosse game was fun, and the dinner out with all the roommates gave you some fresh insight into how the younger half lives. It means a lot to you that your child is willing to share new friends with you like this, and you know it is a good sign. It hasn't been as hard to adjust to college life as you'd both feared.

You are humming to yourself when you feel the car pull to the right. You steady the wheel but it doesn't take long before you hear a flapping sound coming from the rear of the car on the passenger side. The word *blowout* sears through your mind. The car is even listing a little. And that sound is unmistakable. You must have run over something sharp and blown a tire.

You pull onto the shoulder under an overpass where you are protected from the rain and get out to examine the damage. The lighting is good and you can see the tire clearly. Sure enough, it's down, the wheel almost sitting on the roadway. You feel in your pocket for your cell phone, but it's not there. You check the seat, the glove box, the bags you carried to the car but come up with nothing.

In the trunk is a perfectly good spare, you know, taking mental inventory of the jack and the set of flares in the roadway emergency kit you always carry but never use. But you've never changed a tire yourself. How hard is it? Would someone stop to help? Could you do it yourself if you had to?

You're not in the best shape, you know. You made all those plans to raise your fitness level, increase your stamina, and boost your strength, but you didn't follow through on any of them, and now you sure wish you had. But all you can do now is promise you will tomorrow.

Someone is bound to come along, you figure. In the meantime, you'll do your best. You get out the jack, the flare, the lug wrench, the spare. You put on your flashers. You set up your super emergency flashlight. You take off your jacket and roll up your sleeves. You can read; you can follow directions; you can figure out how to change the tire.

But you sure wish you knew for sure you could turn the lug wrench.

Getting Stronger With the Right Routine

As we grow older, fitness experts recommend weight training as the optimal method of improving body strength, enhancing physical appearance, and thwarting the aging process. You can set up a weight training area in your home to help combat the normal decline in muscle mass that begins in middle age, and with proper training you can reach levels of strength beyond any you achieved in your youth. Biologically, our bodies begin to decline about 1 percent a year at age thirty-five, but this natural weakening can be lessened and even reversed through regular exercise.

How does exercise do this for us? It rejuvenates the lungs and heart, makes the muscles and bones stronger, elevates our mood and changes our attitudes about what we can accomplish. Experiments have shown that even very elderly people between the ages of eighty-five and ninety-five grew strong enough through an eight-week exercise program to lift weights that were three times as heavy as those they could lift when they began the program.

Life expectancy today has increased dramatically. At age sixty-five, women can expect to live an average of nineteen more years and men fifteen, compared to an average lifespan of seventy-five years in 1950 and forty-seven years in 1900. Certainly heredity and simple good fortune have a lot to do with how long we live. But the factors within our control—good nutrition, proper rest, and regular exercise—can and should be used to lengthen our life and improve its quality.

Studies show that exercise can actually turn back the clock if a rigorous, well-planned regimen is followed. Even a moderate level decreases the chances of stroke, heart attack, cancer, and other chronic diseases by lowering blood pressure, enlarging the diameter of arteries, improving digestion, strengthening bones, and revving up metabolism. Clinical studies have shown that people who are forced to endure even a month of bedrest often show a decline in both muscle function and lung and heart capacity.

To get started on a weight training program at home, visit your local sports store and ask for help selecting a set of dumbbells. These are short bars with a weight attached at each end that come in a variety of colors and grips. Start small, with hand weights of two or five pounds each. Don't purchase weights that feel too heavy. As a rule of thumb, pick a weight you can lift eight but not more than twelve times. It is more effective for building strength and stamina to do more repetitions at a lower weight than fewer at a higher one.

You don't have to hire a personal trainer to set up a weight-training routine, though a few lessons at the gym can be a good idea to get started. Just check your local library for instruction books appropriate to your level of fitness. Figure on a weight routine of fifteen minutes three times a week to start. Your routine should include at least one exercise in each of the four major categories: upper body pushing, upper body pulling, lower body compound movement, and trunk or midsection exercise. The goal is to hoist, tote, or lift against resistance, which means working against gravity.

Exercises to Lower Your Biological Age

All exercise routines should begin with stretching and warming up movements to tone muscles and improve flexibility and coordination and end with a similar cool-down session. Stretch slowly and gently for five to ten minutes. Your workout should also contain an aerobic or movement component to stimulate the cardiovascular system. Try to do this form of exercise five days a week for at least twenty minutes.

What constitutes a good aerobic workout? You are succeeding in your workout if you break a sweat. You can walk or jog, hike, dance, bike, swim, or play tennis. For some people a brisk run with the family pet is all the exercise they need. Fitness experts define aerobic exercise as any activity that makes you breathe deeply, uses the thigh and buttocks muscles, lasts at least twenty minutes without a break and keeps your pulse between 50 and 60 percent of your maximal heart rate.

To find your maximal heart rate, simply subtract your age from 220. For example, if you are fifty years old, your maximal heart rate is 170. To see whether you've hit your zone, take your pulse for ten seconds after a workout and multiply by six. At age fifty your zone would be 85 to 102 beats per minute (50 percent of 170 equals 85; 60 percent of 170 equals 102). As you improve and become more fit, you could raise your zone to 60 to 85 percent.

One way to gain the benefits of exercise without feeling the pinch of a routine is to train yourself to park blocks away from your destination and walk. Leave your car on the far side of the shopping mall, for example, or select a parking spot half a mile from your office. As you go up to your office, skip the elevator and take the stairs.

Studies from the Centers for Disease Control in Atlanta show that 66 percent of Americans do not exercise enough to protect their health, and 42 percent are completely sedentary. If you are one of these people, try getting into an exercise routine by making it fun. One way to do this is to get involved with a neighborhood walking group, or if you can't find one start one yourself. Adding a social or entertainment component to your exercise plan will help you meet your fitness goals. You can also use music or TV programming as a motivator, particularly if you work out on a treadmill or stationary bike at home.

THE THREE MYTHS OF AGING

Do our perceptions of people in middle age match their actual status? Do our expectations of the elderly adequately reflect their real abilities? Often the answer to both these questions is no. In truth, our society is mired in denial about some of the most important truths about aging. Look at these three commonly held beliefs and see for yourself.

Myth #1: As you age, you are likely to become ill. Not so! Society is often obsessed with the negative rather than the positive aspects of aging. Today's middle-aged population shows a dramatic reduction in high blood pressure, high cholesterol, and smoking, the three most common precursors to the chronic diseases that cut short a major percentage of lives a generation ago.

Myth #2: You can't broaden or sharpen your mind when you grow older. Wrong again. Research shows that while the limits of learning do become more restricted as we age, they can be expanded to almost optimal performance if the right conditions exist. Research is currently being done to determine those conditions and educate schools and work organizations on how to implement them.

Myth #3: Older people's ability to reduce risk and promote health is primarily genetically determined and out of our control. Absolutely not. Choosing one's parents'wisely is not only way we can boost our longevity, and new research is showing that many age-related changes are not irreversible. Increased awareness of the need for good nutrition and high levels of fitness continue to prolong good health, and it is never too late to begin to practice healthy habits and see lifelong improvement in our health and well-being.

Developing Nutrition Know-How

Why do we gain weight as we age, and what can we do about it? We begin to seriously lose muscle fiber in our thirties, and each decade we live we typically lose about six more pounds of muscle. At the same time, however, our fat volume is rising, and even if our weight is the same at fifty as it was at thirty, we will have proportionately more fat than muscle. And that means we need fewer calories, because it takes less food energy to maintain fat tissue.

This causes our bodies to naturally shift to a lower metabolism, but few of us alter our eating habits to adjust to the change. By the time we realize what's going on, we have gained pounds that are difficult to shed. This results in a nation where between 50 and 60 percent of us are overweight.

Beware of the Freshman Fifteen! That's the weight gain our kids often experience as they begin college—and the gain we can expect if we don't adjust to our decreased metabolism by changing our eating habits. This is most easily accomplished with better nutritional awareness. Dieticians today recommend that after age forty, people follow a calorie-counting regimen based on multiplying their body weight by fourteen.

For example, if you weigh 150 pounds, you would need 2100 calories to maintain your weight. To gain a pound, you must ingest an additional 3500 calories, and to lose a pound you will have to consume 3500 fewer calories than you need. This may sound like an awful lot, but look at it this way: If you want to lose a pound a week, simply cut out 500 calories a day. This number times seven will eliminate 3500 calories from your diet per week.

Once your child is off to college, you should rid your cupboards of the cookies, cakes, and candies you kept on hand for all the hungry teenagers who dropped by unexpectedly. Remove temptation from your path! High-calorie goodies may be fine for kids, but for those of us in our middle years they can lead to unwanted pounds we might never be able to shed.

New Research for Healthier Diets

Recent scientific inquiry on fat consumption shows that eating fat is not the major cause of weight gain, as was previously believed. The rate of obesity in American adults has increased over the last decade, while the percentage of fat in the typical diet has declined. How can this be? While many people have followed nutritionists' advice and reduced their consumption of red meat, butter, and whole milk, they have made up for the missing calories by eating more of everything else, much of it low-fat food.

Unfortunately, these low-fat foods contain as many calories as the ones they were designed to replace, since many manufacturers compensate for the loss of taste by adding extra sugar. Hence a return to the cardinal rule of dieting: If you want to lose weight, curb your calories.

Although nutritional advice is always being fine-tuned to fit with the latest scientific discovery, certain basic tenets of healthy eating remain true. These include trying to get most of your carbohydrate allotment from fresh fruit and vegetables and foods rich in complex carbohydrates, especially whole grains, rice, and pasta, and reducing your intake of processed carbohydrates like sugary pastries as much as possible.

Whole grains are especially healthful, as they have been found to help reduce the risk of heart disease and diabetes. Nutritional experts say it's best to get as much of your protein as possible from plant sources, like soy products, beans, and whole wheat bread plus low-fat dairy products. Consume healthy oils and fats in the form of olive oil and raw nuts, such as walnuts, almonds, and macadamia nuts.

RESOURCES FOR INCREASING VIGOR AND WELL-BEING

Online sources of health information can be your best bet for finding out what's so new it hasn't had time to be printed yet and for ferreting out basic material as well. These websites will provide you with up-to-date fitness, nutrition, and medical information and keep you posted on new research as it develops.

Current and archived articles from Harvard Medical School's five nationally respected health publications can be found at *www. harvardhealthpubs.org.* Gain timely and reliable news from *The Harvard Health Letter, The Harvard Heart Letter, The Harvard Women's Health Watch, The Harvard Men's Health Watch,* and *The Harvard Mental Health Letter* at this website.

The former Surgeon General of the United States, C. Everett Koop, M.D., created the website *www.shapeup.org* to promote healthy weight and higher levels of physical activity. Find out about new fitness programs, scientific guidelines for weight loss, and nutrition news.

Look into *www.nejm.org* to read the prestigious *New England Journal of Medicine* each month. Get cutting edge news and editorial commentary in the medical field at the same time as health professionals.

Trust the major center for sleep research at Stanford University to maintain a huge volume of up-to-date information at *www. Stanford.edu/~dement/* to help you find a wide range of material on sleep disorders, dream research, and sleep labs.

Many of us will develop cholesterol issues as we grow older, and new research has shown that in addition to lowering our consumption of egg yolks and red meat, we can help reduce our cholesterol levels by consuming five to ten grams a day of soluble fiber from fruits and vegetables and twenty-five grams a day of soy protein.

If you don't want to give up meat, today's nutritionists say you should consider eating chicken or cold-water fish several times a week and reduce your intake of red meat as much as possible. Research has long linked red meat to coronary disease, and recent findings have begun to suggest a relationship between red meat consumption and osteoporosis. If you do eat meat, however, grilling it is better than frying in terms of limiting fats.

"N" Is for Nutrient

Many people believe that vitamins can boost the immune system, lower cholesterol levels, reduce the risk of heart attack and even slow the aging process. As we age, however, our bodies become less efficient in absorbing nutrients due to natural changes in the way we digest food. Nutritionists estimate that only 10 to 15 percent of people over forty fully absorb sufficient vitamins and minerals from their food to prevent nutritional deficiencies. They recommend taking supplements in the form of high-quality vitamin pills to increase the chances that these essential nutrients reach our bloodstream in sufficient doses.

To boost your ability to gain from the supplements you take, nutritionists suggest trying to lower your intake of caffeine, alcohol, and highly processed carbohydrates. Smoking and stress also interfere with absorption.

It is possible, however, to get too much of a good thing. Research conducted by the National Academy of Sciences, for example, has demonstrated that there is an upper limit for the intake of calcium, a mineral that is increasingly being added to common foods like orange juice. If you take a daily calcium supplement, watch your milligrams and don't increase your risk of kidney damage by going over 2500. At age fifty, men need about 1200 milligrams a day, women about 1500.

The U.S. Department of Agriculture's Human Nutrition Research Center on Aging suggests that age-related changes can be slowed by increasing our intake of specific nutrients in the middle years. These include vitamins E, C, and beta carotene, a form of vitamin A, all members of what is known as the antioxidant family. Antioxidants do their work by preventing loose electrons, called free radicals, from damaging our cells.

In beta carotene studies, the risk of heart attack and stroke were shown to be cut in half for men who consumed twenty-five milligrams of the nutrient daily. This is the equivalent of about a cup of cooked carrots. In another study vitamin C was deemed responsible for preventing some diabetes complications and reducing the buildup of sugars in the body that are believed to cause cataracts.

Vitamin E was shown to reduce the risk of cancer in one study and to aid the immune system in people over fifty. Even at levels currently recommended by the National Academy of Sciences—eight to ten milligrams a day—the vitamin helped build red blood cells and fortify disease-fighting white blood cells. Levels used in experiments reached many times the recommended daily amount.

Sleep Now, Age Later

In addition to good nutrition and proper fitness, getting enough sleep makes us look younger, feel more energized, and think more clearly. As such it has the capacity to add years of good health to our lives. Yet the National Commission on Sleep Disorders states emphatically that one in three Americans does not get enough sleep.

Lack of sufficient sleep not only prevents us from feeling our best, it can actually be dangerous. According to the Journal of the American Medical Association, 13 percent of car accidents are caused by people who fall asleep at the wheel, and severe insomnia is considered a major factor in the onset of depression of close to eight million Americans.

Sleep deprivation causes wear and tear on our cells, decreasing cell-repair rates and lowering our ability to synthesize proteins. While we sleep, arterial blood pressure falls, heart rate decreases, muscles relax, and the blood vessels of our skin dilate. Our immune system gets a boost and our body produces human growth hormone, a substance that is currently being marketed for its antiaging properties.

Although we don't always realize it, our need for sleep changes as we age. Studies have shown that the average twenty-five-year-old feels best after sleeping eight to nine hours a night, but most fifty-year-olds need only seven to eight hours. Much of our need for sleep is determined by heredity. If your parents needed more than the average amount of sleep, chances are so will you.

What should you do if you want to sleep but just can't seem to do so? Sleep experts recommend a variety of remedies for simple insomnia. One of the most effective is learning to put your worries aside. This is often easier said than done, of course, but here's one method that has been shown to work.

Find some paper and a pen and write down each worry on a separate piece of paper, fold up each piece, and put them all away in a specially designated worry box. The box can be anything from a simple shoebox to a beautifully crafted stained glass container. The gesture helps rid your mind of the kind of anxiety that keeps the adrenaline flowing. Often the physical act of putting your worries away helps banish them from your mind and encourages feelings of peacefulness that lead to sleep.

Another technique that many people find helpful is creative visualization. As you lie in bed, try to envision a beautiful place. It could be the site of last summer's vacation, a place you've seen in a magazine ad, or even a fantasy scene you design yourself. In your mind's eye create a sense of calm and beauty and then place yourself at its center. It is like creating an instant dream, and you will feel your body relax.

Remember counting sheep? A variation on this old-fashioned sleep aid is to find something familiar to count, such as pairs of shoes in your closet or numbers of seats in a commuter train. Or you can do a free count starting from zero or start at one hundred and count backwards, visualizing one item for each number and placing your hand holding up each number in red as the items move before your eyes. Chances are you will be asleep before you know it.

SLUMBER CLINIC: HOW MUCH REST DO YOU NEED?

If you awaken feeling sluggish most mornings or find yourself wishing for a nap during the day, it's possible you need more rest. To determine whether you are getting less sleep than your body requires, try this simple test.

Choose a bedtime that will enable you to sleep for eight hours and still get up on time for work in the morning. Go to bed at that same time every night for a week. At the end of the week, note your responses. Did you need an alarm clock to wake you up? Were you tired during the day? Was it hard to get out of bed in the morning? If the answer is yes to any of these questions, you are not getting enough sleep.

To remedy the situation, try going to bed half an hour earlier at night. Stick to this new bedtime for a week, then ask yourself the same three questions. If the answer to any one is still yes, adjust your bedtime back another fifteen minutes. Repeat the steps for another week until you find yourself awakening refreshed without an alarm clock and staying alert all day.

Chapter
Twenty

COMING HOME AGAIN:
VACATIONS AND VISITS

You've stocked the fridge, cooked all your child's favorite dishes, and hung the welcome home sign across the mantle. Now there's nothing to do but wait until it's time to go to the airport and meet the plane.

You fluff the sofa pillows in the den one more time, then look around the room, aware for the first time that you're feeling a bit frazzled. It's not that everything isn't in its place; its just that some of the places have changed in the months since your child first left and catapulted you into another dimension.

You've moved the computer upstairs, for example, and canceled the cable TV subscription. The dining room table, polished and shiny now that it is no longer covered with homework, is beautifully decorated by a bouquet of silk flowers in all your favorite colors. Even the birdcage, a fixture in the living room corner for so many years, has been moved to the garage since the parakeet went to its final reward several months ago. Did you announce its demise to your college freshman? You can't remember. Oh, well, you hope it won't spoil the homecoming.

There is just enough time for a cup of tea, and while the warm liquid settles your stomach you realize it's been so many weeks since you rearranged the kitchen that it no longer looks new or strange to your eye. The table, once in the center, now stands comfortably against the wall, giving you more turning-around space in the room, and you like the change. But will it work when your child is home?

You've fretted for so long it's past time to go, and you shrug into your coat now and worry through your mad dash across town to the airport. Maybe you made too many changes. Maybe the ones you made will make your child feel like a stranger at home. No, you didn't knock down walls or resize windows or pull up the carpeting to expose bare floors. Nothing major has changed. Only everything, you realize, because you don't feel the same inside, and it has nothing whatsoever to do with the furniture or the drapes or the placement of the kitchen table.

But as you run up the ramp to the terminal, you see your child dialing the telephone at the pickup area, no doubt calling to see why you are late, and suddenly you feel your heart stretch all the way across the space and embrace the graceful arms, the curly head, the proud shoulders as if the two of you have never been separated for even a day. Your child looks up and smiles at you, looking old and new and familiar and strange all at the same time. The first holiday visit home from college, and yet another new experience in your life, has begun.

What's a Parent to Do?

It wasn't easy letting go, and for most parents it's certainly no simple task trying to pick up the pieces of a relationship once again after months of separation, growth, and change for all of you. For the lucky ones, the hundreds of e-mails, care packages, and phone calls kept the thread of connection thick and sinewy. But for many families, despite our best efforts, the feelings have grown tentative and the links uncertain. The wish to reach out can be fraught with doubt and sometimes is simply stifled before it has a chance to be expressed.

Is it good to hug a grown child who seems to tower over you now, seemingly four inches taller than you remember? Should you express your affection in a more grown-up manner, shaking hands or gently rapping a shoulder, no matter how broad that shoulder now seems? Should you take your cues from your child and stand back and wait to see how you are approached? Should you ask questions or wait for information to flow on its own impetus? Should you talk about home to fill the gap or leave the gap and hope your child fills it with the college stories you long to hear?

For many parents, the shift in roles away from primary caretaker when college begins can cause enough uncertainty to bring on a major case of inhibition on the first visit home. Even in the best of circumstances we tend to hide our feelings when we are unsure of ourselves; it's just human nature to want to do so when we worry about how our child will react. But from the child's point of view, coming home from college means looking for signs that their new, grown-up selves are welcome.

No matter how independent they may seem, inside most children want reassurance that there is still room for them at home, that there is a place in the family hierarchy for the newly mature person who does not want to follow the old rules but might just be willing, with some negotiation, to fit in in some new, as yet undetermined way. They have changed and grown, for sure, and gaining parental approval for their new selves is of paramount importance to integrating those gains into their psyches in a real way.

Different Families, Similar Issues

Family therapists say it is normal for parents and college-age kids to feel awkward around each other for the first few days at home, often for very different reasons. Some parents who were very involved in their children's activities before they left and who felt they lost an important function in their lives, for example, may not have completely mourned their loss and will find themselves doing so now before they can fully accept that their children are home again, albeit temporarily.

Others who felt constrained by their parenting roles and sprang to life when their child left home may now feel a touch of resentment at the returning burden. Some who felt the loss keenly may experience strong inner warnings to suppress the rising need that would create new entanglements. Still others who made a healthy transition to the new stage of parenting might want to be sure their child has also moved ahead before expressing joy at their own newly reclaimed lives.

There are many issues and not much time to deal with them on most holiday visits. Of paramount importance, though, no matter what the dominant feeling, is to give your child space to find his or her new place in the household. With the watchful eyes and ears with which you listened to your child during the growing-up years, you can now catch the clues that tell you how quickly you can move in trying to reestablish the closeness you long for.

Most of all, be flexible. Back off when the signs tell you to, but do not give up trying to find new ways to make contact when given even the least little bit of encouragement. After all, you are the adult, and no matter how complex the homecoming may seem to you, it is even more emotionally trying for your child.

Under Your Own Roof: How It Feels to Be Back

What is your child experiencing upon entering the homestead once again? Relief, for sure, that you and your home are still there, regardless of whether the household has been redecorated, reconfigured, or even moved. So much more of our sense of home is rooted in our inner landscape than we realize; the outer trappings of houses and gardens and the other physical places we inhabit are so much less important than the feelings with which we connect when our sense of security is intact.

Many homecoming students will be eager to share new experiences with parents and siblings; others will seem strangely distant for hours, even days, until they move back into the skins that were shed when they first left home. For some, the most important event will seem to be getting together with old high school friends, providing that all-important chance to measure themselves against the person they were before they left.

Don't be disappointed, however, if your child's interest in family events seems small or even nonexistent at first. Despite the fact that your son or daughter will likely run out the door soon after coming home, don't be deceived by this behavior. Sooner or later all the old friends will be visited and all the notes will be compared and the primacy of family will once again reassert itself. You are still the center of the universe, the key person your child leaves and the one to whom he or she returns; you have not lost your place or your importance.

Kids attending college near home may return to the roost for a short visit in the fall, but most will not be back until the Thanksgiving weekend or even the long winter holiday break. But even if school is only an hour from home, kids often feel they've been on a different planet once they step back into the confines of family life. The truth is in some ways they have been living in a foreign country for the months they have been away, and coming home can feel very much like culture shock. International students who choose to study far from home say they adapt to their new environment surprisingly quickly; it is going back to their home country, no matter how much they love it, that is the more difficult adjustment.

College students, freshmen especially, dream of freshly cooked meals, clean sheets, and privacy in the bathroom for all the months they are away at school. It can be difficult meeting their expectations when they are back in the nest once again, no matter how hard you try, because often home takes on a larger-than-life quality while they are away. At the same time that the freshman experience makes them pull away from us to help buoy their shaky sense of independence, they tend to romanticize their old lives in ways that can make reality fall short of their memories when they meet them face-to-face on holiday visits.

QUIZ: ARE YOU READY FOR HOMECOMING?

Whether it's fall break, Thanksgiving vacation, winter holiday, spring break, or even summer vacation, you can help pave the way for a warm and happy visit by equipping yourself for the task ahead. Test your preparedness by answering these ten questions. Give yourself ten points for each yes answer, then check your score at the end to see where you stand on the one-hundred-point readiness scale.

1. Can you live for several weeks with someone in the house who sleeps all day and parties all night?
2. If your child comes home with piercings or green hair, have you thought of an appropriate response?
3. If you don't live near public transportation, will you be willing and able to share your car?
4. Have you and your spouse discussed household rules and dis-

cipline so you are ready to talk to your child about expected behavior?

5. Have you informed your friends, relatives and coworkers that you will be unreachable by phone for the duration of the vacation because the phone will be busy every minute of every day?

6. Can you deal with a child who has become a strict vegetarian or announces an ardent allegiance to a political party of which you highly disapprove?

7. If you have converted your child's room to a den, home office, or exercise room, have you set up an alternative sleeping area that will make him or her happy and comfortable?

8. Have you arranged to take sufficient time off from work to spend with your child during his or her vacation?

9. Even if your refrigerator is full right now, are you prepared to take several unplanned trips to the supermarket to restock it?

10. Are you able to give up using your home computer during the visit, since it will probably be appropriated with college e-mail 24-7?

If you scored ninety to one hundred points, congratulations—you belong to a very small group of open-minded, well-organized, progressive parents! A score of sixty to eighty points falls within the range of normal folks who love their kids but are still working hard to adjust to this new stage of parenthood. Scores of fifty points and below show a need to do some more planning to avoid being overwhelmed by the host of late-adolescent issues that plague the college years but also make them a time of tremendous growth and excitement for students and parents alike.

Starting Over Setting Rules

Once again, it is up to you as the adult to help create a balance between family unity and individual independence. Old patterns of behavior need not be continued exactly as they were when your child still lived at home; new rules should be discussed and agreed upon as soon as possible. It is a good idea to sit down with your spouse a few days before the visit is scheduled and talk about your current household routines. Most likely in the months your child has been away at college you have altered the ways your home functions. Spend some

CHECKLIST: A NECESSARY VACATION CONVERSATION

Kids away on their own for the first time need you to give them freedom but watch over them at the same time. While it can take several tries to achieve the right balance, one way to accomplish this is to let them make their own decisions while at school but guide them carefully when they come home. To make sure kids are on the right track, sit down together and discuss each of these questions. If it feels too awkward to speak in person, write a letter and ask for a written response.

1. Are the students in your dorm very involved with alcohol?
2. Are communications with home taking place often enough? Too often?
3. Do you feel you are in the right school?
4. Are there any doctors you would like to visit while you are home?
5. Are you able to handle your homework load?
6. Do you like the people around you at school?
7. Are your physically comfortable in your surroundings?
8. Do you always feel safe on campus?
9. Are you learning enough?
10. Are you having fun?

time now to enumerate them and discuss how they will be affected once your child comes home.

For example, do you go to bed and get up at the same time as before? Do you shop at the supermarket as often? Do you like to linger in the kitchen now with a second cup of coffee in the morning? Do you prefer the TV and stereo turned off by a certain hour? Do you have the same number of cars as before? Perhaps the changes have been so natural and so gradual you didn't notice, but you are sure to run smack into them when your child becomes part of the picture once again.

Make a list of sensitive areas and decide with your spouse where you are willing to compromise and what is too important to you to give up. For example, if music playing in the next room won't disturb your sleep, that's fine. But if you need to rise at 6:00 A.M. to get ready for work and you can't sleep with noise, you would be wise to discuss this with your visiting child the evening before, not the morning after.

Waking up to an empty refrigerator when you need a good break-fast for the day ahead can be avoided with some advance planning. And you can be certain that the entire concept of curfew will need to be reintroduced to a child used to living in an environment where no one is keeping tabs.

Always try to keep in mind that dorm life bears little resemblance to normal family life. Your child has developed new rhythms, new tol-erances, and new desires you are sure to find incompatible with your own. Discuss them early on in the visit and try to head off trouble be-fore it begins by asking your child what he or she would like, express-ing your wishes, and compromising where you can. Just as when your teenager was still living at home, setting restrictions together rather than imposing your preset standards will help insure that the rules are followed.

Uninvited Guests and Other Vacation Surprises

All parents are happy to hear that their children have made new friends and found a circle of interesting people with whom to share the wealth of new experiences. But not all are filled with glee at the prospect of housing one or three or six of these new friends for a hol-iday visit, especially if they were secretly looking forward to time alone to share friendly family intimacies with their visiting child.

What should you do if your college freshman walks in the front door and announces that a special friend or even a small troupe of buddies wants to camp out on the living room floor? Even if you are one of those generous parents who is likely to invite them in to stay, you can make the experience much more pleasant by gauging your child's motivation and making a plan to act appropriately.

First of all, allow yourself to feel flattered that your child thinks so highly of you and the home you provide that he or she is willing to share them with friends. It is a sign of both a good family relationship and psychological health on the part of the student that the two dis-parate worlds of school and home can be bridged in this manner. Only children who are well-adjusted and comfortable in both old and new venues will risk combining them. Simply put, children who have something to hide do not bring their friends home to mom and dad for scrutiny.

Next determine the nature of the relationships among the visitors. Is your child dating the guest, for example, or if there is a group of kids do you feel that any of the relationships is sexually charged? If you can't determine this on your own, ask your child openly; even though it can seem difficult, it is far easier than awakening in the middle of the night to behavior that will make you uncomfortable. Bringing it out in the open now, before it happens, is less embarrassing for everyone and allows for a degree of control that will no longer be possible once it progresses too far.

Creating Structure and Support

Be assertive in setting ground rules that you can live with. Speak in private with your child and let him or her tell the others your wishes. Are you prepared to feed the visitors? You certainly can if you have the time and inclination, but you are not duty-bound to do so. Nor do you have to provide laundry service or even the use of your washing machine if you don't want to. Saying no before you are asked is much easier than trying to wiggle out of a potentially awkward situation later on.

On the other hand, if you have been suffering from having no one to nurture, a houseful of kids might be just the ticket to fill your parenting cup once again. If that is so, cook and launder and entertain your way to feeling useful and needed and give those kids a wonderful, homey vacation. Along the way you are sure to hear a lot of new stories, see firsthand how your child is perceived, and learn a great deal about his or her new life. Viewed this way, company can feel like a special gift to you and a way to share your child's life on a deeper level.

SHORT ANSWERS FOR LONG HOLIDAY BREAKS

It's not difficult to find lots of worthwhile activities to fill short visits, especially those that center around family holidays like Thanksgiving. But winter breaks typically last between four and six weeks, and these longer periods at home for students who are used to being busy all the time can send families straight into chaos. Here are some ideas to help you mount an antilounge campaign, keep your household humming at a healthy rhythm, and provide your student with engaging work.

Take a course at a local college. Many universities run January sessions to help students get a jump on next semester's courses or make up one missed in the fall. With advance permission from your child's college, he or she can attend class and gain credits in a chosen discipline.

Find a seasonal job at a local department store. Shops often need help for both holiday sales and January inventory, and with part-time temporary employment your child can pick up some extra spending money to take back to college for the spring semester.

Work on a community service project. If a volunteer position provided a sense of accomplishment during the high school years, odds are the organization will be happy to have an experienced, mature worker come back to lend a hand once again for several weeks.

Teach computer skills to local seniors. Whether college kids give private lessons or visit senior centers to provide group instruction, older people will be happy to learn how to use computers and gain mastery over software programs.

Become an elementary school reader. Many teachers appreciate college students who volunteer to read to groups of children while they work with other students in need of individual attention. Kids love to meet older kids who graduated from their school, and college students will feel in a very real way just how much they've grown.

BIBLIOGRAPHY

Part I: Love in a Time of Transition

Adams, Jane. *I'm Still Your Mother: How to Get Along With Your Grown-Up Children for the Rest of Your Life*. New York: Delacorte Press, 1994.

Atkins, Dale. *Sisters*. New York: Arbor House, 1984.

Beisser, Arnold. *The Only Gift: Thoughts on the Meaning of Friends and Friendship*. New York: Doubleday, 1991.

Carter, Betty, and Joan Peters. *Love, Honor and Negotiate: Making Your Marriage Work*. New York: Simon & Schuster, 1996.

Coburn, Karen, and Marge Treeger. *Letting Go: A Parents' Guide to Today's College Experience, Third Edition*. Bethesda, Md.: Adler & Adler, 1998.

Duck, Steve. *Friends, for Life: The Psychology of Close Relationships*. New York: St. Martin's Press, 1983.

Gillies, Jerry. *Friends: The Power and Potential of the Company You Keep*. New York: Coward, McCann & Geoghegan, 1976.

Goodman, Ellen. "Parental Connections." *The Syracuse Post-Standard*, 19, Sept. 1997: A-19.

Gottman, John, and Nan Silver. *The Seven Principles for Making Marriage Work*. New York: Three Rivers Press, 2000.

Greenberg, Vivian. *Children of a Certain Age: Adults and Their Aging Parents*. New York: Lexington Books, 1994.

Hendrix, Harville. *Getting the Love You Want: A Guide for Couples*. New York: Henry Holt & Co., 1998.

Hersh, Richard. "Intentions and Perceptions: A National Survey of Public Attitudes Towards Liberal Arts Education." *Change* March–April 1997, pp. 42–44.

Kennedy, Eugene. *On Being a Friend*. New York: Continuum, 1982.

Klagsbrun, Francine. *Mixed Feelings: Love, Hate, Rivalry and Reconciliation Among Brothers and Sisters*. New York: Bantam Books, 1982.

_____. *Married People: Staying Together in an Age of Divorce*. New York: Bantam Books, 1985.

Kramer, Judy. *Changing Places: A Journey With My Parents Into Their Old Age*. New York: Penguin Putnam, 2000.

Krasnow, Iris. *Surrendering to Marriage: Husbands, Wives and Other Imperfections*. New York: Miramax Books, 2001.

Leder, Jane Mersky. *Brothers and Sisters: How They Shape Our Lives*. New York: St. Martin's Press, 1991.

McGraw, Phillip. *Relationship Rescue: A Seven-Step Strategy for Reconnecting With Your Partner*. New York: Hyperion, 2000.

Merrell, Susan Scarf. *The Accidental Bond: The Power of Sibling Relationships*. New York: Random House, 1995.

Moore, Thomas. *Soul Mates: Honoring the Mysteries of Love and Relationships*. New York: HarperCollins, 1994.

Pipher, Mary. *Another Country: Navigating the Emotional Terrain of Our Elders*. New York: Riverhead Books, 1999.

Pogrebin, Letty Cottin. *Getting Over Getting Older: An Intimate Journey*. New York: Little, Brown & Co., 1996.

Rubin, Lillian. *Just Friends: The Role of Friendship in Our Lives*. New York: HarperCollins, 1985.

Schiff, Harriet Sarnoff. *How Did I Become My Parent's Parent?* New York: Viking Penguin, 1996.

Unell, Barbara, and Jerry Wyckoff. *The Eight Seasons of Parenthood: How the Stages of Parenting Constantly Reshape Our Adult Identities*. New York: Random House, 2000.

Wallerstein, Judith, and Sandra Blakeslee. *The Good Marriage: How and Why Love Lasts*. Boston: Houghton Mifflin & Co., 1995.

Part II: New Freedom, Fresh Joy

Amabile, Teresa. *Growing Up Creative: Nurturing a Lifetime of Creativity*. New York: Crown, 1989.

Blakeslee, Thomas. *The Right Brain: A New Understanding of the Unconscious Mind and Its Creative Powers*. Garden City, N.Y.: Doubleday, 1980.

Carroll, Andrew. *Volunteer USA*. New York: Fawcett Columbine, 1991.

Devney, Darcy Campion. *The Volunteers Survival Manual: The Only Practical Guide to Giving Your Time and Money*. Cambridge, Mass.: The Practical Press, 1992.

Downs, Hugh. *Fifty to Forever*. Nashville, Tenn.: Thomas Nelson Publishers, 1994.

Driver, David. *The Good Heart Book: A Guide to Volunteering*. Chicago: The Noble Press, 1989.

Duper, Linda Leeb. *160 Ways to Help the World: Community Service Projects for Young People*. New York: Facts on File, 1996.

Edwards, Betty. *Drawing on the Right Side of the Brain: A Course in Enhancing Creativity and Artistic Confidence*. Los Angeles: J. P. Tarcher, Inc., 1979.

Friedman, Bonnie. *Writing Past Dark: Envy, Fear, Distraction and Other Dilemmas in the Writer's Life*. New York: HarperCollins, 1993.

Grout, Pam. *Art & Soul: 156 Ways to Free Your Creative Spirit*. Kansas City, Mo.: Andrews McMeel Publishing, 2000.

Hunt, Bernice, and Morton Hunt. *Prime Time: A Guide to the Pleasures and Opportunities of the New Middle Age*. New York: Stein and Day, 1975.

Jonas, Doris, and David Jonas. *Young Till We Die*. New York: Coward, McCann & Geoghegan, Inc., 1973.

Kimbrough, John. *The Vacation Home Exchange and Hospitality Guide*. Fresno, Calif.: Kimco Communications, 1991.

Lanier, Pamela. *The Complete Guide to Condo Vacations, Seventh Edition*. Petaluma, Calif.: Lanier Publishing International, 1998.

May, Rollo. *The Courage to Create*. New York: W.W. Norton & Company, 1975.

McGuckin, Frank, ed. *Volunteerism*. New York: H.W. Wilson Company, 1998.

Rubin, Lillian. *Women of a Certain Age: The Midlife Search for Self*. New York: HarperCollins, 1979.

Wall, Ginita, and Victoria Collins. *Your Next Fifty Years*. New York: Henry Holt & Co., 1997.

Part III: More Power on the Job

Applegath, John. *Working Free: Practical Alternatives to the Nine-to-Five Job*. New York: Amacom, 1982.

Bolles, Richard. *What Color Is Your Parachute?* Berkeley, Calif.: Ten-Speed Press, 1996.

Crane, Shena. *What Do I Do Now? Making Sense of Today's Changing Workplace*. Irvine, Calif.: Vista Press, 1994.

Doyle, Robert. *Essential Skills and Strategies in the Helping Process*. Pacific Grove, Calif.: Brooks Cole, 1992.

Dwyer, Don. *Target Success: How You Can Become a Successful Entrepreneur, Regardless of Your Background*. Holbrook, Mass.: Bob Adams Publishers, 1993.

Edwards, Paul, and Sarah Edwards. *Finding Your Perfect Work: The New Career Guide to Making a Living, Creating a Life*. New York: G.P. Putnam's Sons, 1996.

_____. *Working From Home: Everything You Need to Know About Living and Working Under the Same Roof*. Los Angeles: J. P. Tarcher, Inc., 1987.

Fisher, Anne. *If My Career's on the Fast Track, Where Do I Get a Road Map? Surviving and Thriving in the Real World of Work*. New York: William Morrow, 2001.

Goldman, Katherine Wise. *If You Can Raise Kids, You Can Get a Good Job*. New York: HarperCollins, 1996.

Helfand, David P. *Career Change: Everything You Need to Know to Meet New Challenges and Take Control of Your Career, Second Edition*. Chicago: VGM Career Horizons, 1999.

Hingston, Peter. *Starting Your Own Business*. New York: Dorling Kindersley, 2001.

Hirsch, Arlene. *Love Your Work and Success Will Follow*. New York: John Wiley & Sons, 1996.

Lucht, John. *Executive Job-Changing Workbook*. New York: Viceroy, 1994.

Maul, Lyle, and Dianne Mayfield. *The Entrepreneur's Road Map to Business Success*. Los Angeles: Saxtons River Publications, 1990.

Miner, John. *The Four Routes to Entrepreneurial Success*. San Francisco: Berrett-Koehler Publishers, 1996.

Moreau, Daniel. *Take Charge of Your Career: Survive and Profit From a Mid-Career Change*. New York: Random House, 1996.

Parker, Julie. *Careers for Women in the Clergy*. New York: Rosen Publishing Group, 1993.

Robertson, Arthur, and William Proctor. *Work a Four-Hour Day: Achieving Business Efficiency on Your Own Terms*. New York: Avon Books, 1994.

Sharma, Poonam. *The Harvard Entrepreneurs Club Guide to Starting Your Own Business*. New York: John Wiley & Sons, 1999.

Sher, Barbara. *I Could Do Anything . . . If I Only Knew What It Was: How to Discover What You Really Want and How to Get It*. New York: Dell, 1994.

————. *It's Only Too Late If You Don't Start Now: How to Create Your Second Life at Any Age*. New York: Dell, 1999.

Shertzer, Bruce, and Shelly Stone. *Fundamentals of Counseling*. Boston: Houghton Mifflin, 1994.

Simmons, Terri. *How to Own and Operate Your Home Day Care Business Successfully Without Going Nuts!* Phoenix, Ariz.: Amber Books, 1999.

U.S. Department of Labor. *Occupational Outlook Handbook*. Washington, D.C.: Government Printing Office, 2000.

Part IV: Family Finance Reform

Altfest, Lewis J., and Karen Altfest. *Lew Altfest Answers Almost All Your Questions About Money*. New York: McGraw-Hill, 1992.

Brill, Jack, and Alan Reder. *Investing From the Heart: The Guide to Socially Responsible Investments and Money Management*. New York: Crown Publishers, 1992.

Gardner, David, and Tom Gardner. *The Motley Fool Investment Workbook.* New York: Simon & Schuster, 1998.

Jaffe, David. *The New College Financial Aid System.* Chicago: Council Oaks Books, 2000.

Jurinski, James John. *Keys to Preparing a Will.* Hauppauge, N.Y.: Barron's Educational Series, 1998.

Krefetz, Gerald. *Paying for College: A Guide for Parents.* Princeton, N.J.: The College Board, 1996.

Leider, Robert, and Anna Leider. *Lovejoy's Guide to Financial Aid.* New York: Simon & Schuster, 2001.

Lieberman, Trudy. *Life Insurance: How to Buy the Right Policy from the Right Company at the Right Price.* New York: Consumer Reports Books, 1998.

Light, Richard J. *Making the Most of College: Students Speak Their Minds.* Cambridge, Mass.: Harvard University Press, 2001.

Longman, Phillip. "The Cost of Children." *U.S. News & World Report* 30 March 1998: 16.

Malkiel, Burton. *A Random Walk Down Wall Street: The Best Investment Advice for the New Century.* New York: W. W. Norton & Co, 1999.

Margolin, Judith. *Financing a College Education.* New York: Plenum Press, 1996.

Miller, Matthew. "$140,000—and a Bargain." *The New York Times Magazine* 13 June 1999: 45.

Nichols, Donald. *Treasury Securities: Making Money with Uncle Sam.* Chicago: Longman Financial Services Publishing, 1990.

Orman, Suze. *The Nine Steps to Financial Freedom.* New York: Crown Publishers, 1997.

Passell, Peter. *Personalized Money Strategies: 15 No-Nonsense Investment Plans to Achieve your Goals.* New York: Warner Books, 1985.

Puner, Linda Pollard. *Starting Out Suburban: A Frosh Year Survival Guide.* Pleasantville, N.Y.: New Forge Press, 1996.

Quinn, Jane Bryant. *Making the Most of Your Money.* New York: Simon & Schuster, 1991.

Root, Jack, and Douglas Mortensen. *The Seven Steps of Financial Success: How to Apply Time-Tested Principles to Create, Manage and Build Personal Wealth.* Homewoood, Ill.: Irwin Publishing Co., 1996.

Shenkman, Martin. *The Estate Planning Guide.* New York: John Wiley & Sons, 1991.

Silver, Don. *A Parent's Guide to Wills and Trusts.* Los Angeles: Adams-Hall Publishing, 1994.

Updegrave, Walter. *How to Keep Your Savings Safe: Protecting the Money You Can't Afford to Lose.* New York: Crown Publishers, 1992.

Vaughn, Emmet. *Fundamentals of Risk and Insurance.* New York: John Wiley & Sons, 1992.

Wachtel, Paul. *The Poverty of Affluence*. Philadelphia: New Society Publishers, 1989.

Part V: Making Your Home Yours Again

Barkin, Carol. *When Your Kid Goes to College: A Parents' Survival Guide*. New York: Avon Books, 1999.

Bloom, Michael V. *Adolescent Parental Separation*. New York: Gardner Press, 1980.

Blos, Peter. *The Adolescent Passage*. New York: International Universities Press, 1979.

Boyer, Ernest. *Campus Life: In Search of Community*. Princeton, N.J.: The Carnegie Foundation for the Advancement of Teaching, 1990.

Cahn, Victor. *A Thinking Student's Guide to College*. Norwell, Mass.: Christopher Publishing House, 1988.

Chase, Chris. *The Great American Waistline: Putting It On and Taking It Off*. New York: Coward, McCann & Geoghegan, 1981.

Cohen, Robert D., ed. *Working With Parents of College Students*. San Francisco: Jossey-Bass Inc., 1985.

Connolly, William. *The New York Times Guide to Buying or Building a Home*. New York: Times Books, 1984.

Cox, Connie, and Cris Evatt. *Thirty Days to a Simpler Life*. New York: Penguin Books, 1998.

Dacyczyn, Amy. *The Tightwad Gazette: Promoting Thrift as a Viable Alternative Lifestyle*. New York: Villard Books, 1993.

Dellabough, Robin. *The Beardstown Ladies' Guide to Smart Spending for Big Savings*. New York: Hyperion, 1997.

Dominguez, Joe, and Vicki Robin. *Your Money or Your Life: Transforming Your Relationship With Money and Achieving Financial Independence*. New York: Penguin Books, 1992.

Elgin, Duane. *Voluntary Simplicity*. New York: William Morrow, 1993.

Grayson, Paul A., and Philip Meilman. *Beating the College Blues, Second Edition*. New York: Checkmark Books, 1999.

Halpern, Howard M. *Cutting Loose: An Adult Guide to Coming to Terms With Parents*. New York: Simon & Schuster, 1976.

Hamilton, Katie, and Gene Hamilton. *Don't Move—Improve!* New York: Henry Holt Books, 1992.

Hamilton, Michael, et al. *The Duke University Medical Center Book of Diet and Fitness*. New York: Fawcett Columbine, 1990.

Horowitz, Helen Lefkowitz. *Campus Life*. New York: Alfred A. Knopf, 1987.

Idzikowski, Chris. *Learn to Sleep Well: A Practical Guide to Getting a Good Night's Rest*. San Francisco: Chronicle Books, 2000.

Janik, Carolyn. *Home-ology*. Washington, D.C.: Kiplinger Books, 1998.

Kaufman, Dr. Richard Clark. *The Age Reduction System: A Complete Program to Help Slow, Halt, or Retard Aging*. New York: Rawson Associates, 1986.

Kenyon, Flip, and Heather Kenyon. *The Smart Money Guide to Buying a Home: Ten Steps to Owning a Great Home and a Great Investment*. Tampa, Fla.: Palladian Publishing, 1999.

Luhrs, Janet. *The Simple Living Guide: A Sourcebook for Less Stressful, More Joyful Living*. New York: Broadway Books, 1997.

McMenamin, Brigid. "The Tyranny of the Diploma." *Forbes* 28 Dec. 1998: 78.

Newman, Barbara, and Philip Newman. *When Kids Go to College: A Parent's Guide to Changing Relationships*. Columbus, Ohio: Ohio State University Press, 1992.

Olinekova, Dr. Gayle. *Power Aging: Staying Young at Any Age*. New York: Thunder's Mouth Press, 1998.

Orme, Alan Dan. *Reviving Old Houses*. Pownal, Vt.: Garden Way Publishing Co., 1989.

Perls, Thomas, and Margery Hutter Silver. *Living to 100: Lessons in Living to Your Maximum Potential at Any Age*. New York: Basic Books, 1999.

Wimsatt, William Upski. "How I Got My Degree at the University of Planet Earth." *Utne Reader* May–June 1998: 23–25.

Woodson, Roger. *The Condo & Co-op Handbook: A Comprehensive Guide to Buying and Owning a Condo or Co-op*. New York: Macmillan, 1998.

INDEX